FINDING
LOVE
IN SPORTS

GROWING IN THE LIKENESS
OF CHRIST

BY ROD HANDLEY & GORDON THIESSEN

BIBLE STUDIES FOR COACHES & ATHLETES

Finding Love in Sports

Rod Handley and Gordon Thiessen

ISBN 978-1-929478-39-2

Cross Training Publishing

www.crosstrainingpublishing.com

(308) 293-3891

Cross Training Publishing

SCAN ME

CONTENTS

CONTACTING THE AUTHORS

Rod Handley
Character That Counts
512 NE Victoria Drive, Lee's Summit, MO 64086
www.characterthatcounts.org

Gordon Thiessen
Cross Training Publishing
15418 Weir Street #177, Omaha, NE 68137
www.crosstrainingpublishing.com

Ron Brown
Kingdom Sports
www.kingdomsports.online

KINGDOM SPORTS MINUTES

Kingdom Sports Minutes are based on Wes Neal's ground-breaking biblical research that impacted the sports-world in the 1970s and inspired Ron Brown and Gordon Thiessen to create resources rooted in Scripture for the Christian athlete and coach over the past three decades.

Our mission is to use sports to help athletes, coaches and parents see their need for King Jesus and serve Him within His Kingdom. Our curricula and resources aim to provide a path for athletes and coaches to become experts in God's design for godly competition. These resources will include books, bible studies, videos, apps and websites. They also provide "hands-on" training opportunities on the fields and courts along with their **Doing Sports God's Way Handbook.**

KINGDOM SPORTS MINUTE

SCAN ME

INTRODUCTION

What is the Fruit of the Spirit Series?

The fruit of the Spirit refers to the nine attributes of a Christian life as defined by the Apostle Paul in his Epistle to the Galatians in the Bible. These attributes are love, joy, peace, patience, kindness, goodness, faithfulness, gentleness, and self-control. They represent the inward change the Holy Spirit brings into the lives of believers. Each of the nine books in this series is designed around these attributes.

Christian coaches and athletes experience significant spiritual growth and transformation, referred to as "fruit" in the Bible. This comparison to fruit-bearing is fitting as these changes reflect the work of God's Spirit within us, producing new behaviors and attitudes. The ultimate goal of this transformation is to bring glory to our Heavenly Father. This transformation is so significant that it is compared to a rebirth, affecting our motivations, curbing sinful habits, and initiating new, righteous ones that will last a lifetime.

How do I use this book?

An easy format to follow is having each person in your group read a paragraph or section of the study before moving to the next person. Don't force anyone to read that would prefer not to do so. Also, make sure each person has a copy of the book in their hands. It's very helpful to have each person reading along with the person who is speaking. There are natural breaks in the study with questions but feel free to add additional comments between paragraphs. Finally, the best practice is to collect all the books and store them for the next meeting. Once you have completed all 16 lessons, you can let the group have the books. That's often easier than allowing them to take the books home each week and expect them to remember to bring them back. However, if you decide to let them keep the books, you will want to have extra book when group members forget to bring their books.

What is "Doing Sports God's Way?"

A summary of Doing Sports God's Way is on page 104. The book is available at Amazon or www.crosstrainingpublishing.com. The book provides a path for athletes and coaches to become experts in God's design for godly competition. Take the Christian Worldview Quiz (page 8) to determine your worldview in sports.

What is Finding Love in Sports story? Finding Love in Sports is an option to introduce the concept of love to your group with The Fellowship of the Unashamed story (page 102).

What is Kingdom Sports Minute?
Each workout has a video from Coach Ron Brown that provides a brief overview of the character trait. You can use your smartphone to scan the QR code and find the video.

What is a Character Attribute Survey?
This is an optional survey (page 73-74) you can use with your group either before or after the workout.

How large should our group be?
This is hard to say, but generally, people feel most comfortable talking and learning in a group of ten or fewer. If your huddle meeting has more than ten, you should break into smaller groups and make sure each person has their own copy of the study. You might consider having a box of books available at each meeting and having the participants pass them back in before they leave each week.

When should we meet?
Groups typically meet during the team's season. The best time to do it is before or after practice, so you are not adding another time commitment to your already busy life.

How can I get the most out of this?
You will get out of this exactly what you put into it. How honest you are with yourself and the others in the group will determine how much you will get out of this. It might be a stretch for some of you to risk being vulnerable for the first time.

Who can lead a group discussion?
The best practice is having an adult or coach lead the study, but depending upon the maturity of the athletes, they can often be effective as small group discussion leaders.

What is a Chapel Talk Outline?
Each study has a talk outline for doing chapels or team talks that last 10 to 15 minutes. When using the study with a group, how large should it be? This is

hard to say, but generally, people feel most comfortable talking and learning in a group of ten or fewer. If your huddle meeting has more than ten, you should break into smaller groups and make sure each person has their own copy of the study. You might consider having a box of books available at each meeting and having the participants pass them back in before they leave each week.

When do I share the Gospel?

The easy answer is, "Whenever you think it's appropriate." Many places in this book describe the Gospel and its impact but feel free to share as you see opportunities. We added the "Step Up to Life" (page 91) diagnostic tool a, along with two presentations used by the Fellowship of Christian Athletes. For many years, I (Gordon Thiessen) used both "Step Up to Life" and the "More Than Winning" (page 95) written by Dave Gibson. I found both approaches helpful when sharing my faith with coaches and athletes. In recent years, FCA has added "The Four" (page 100) to its curriculum to help spread the Gospel. Find something that works for you and use it! You might also find the following question and gospel facts helpful as well.

What is the Gospel?

Christians often say that Jesus died for our sins, but what does that mean? Why did He die? What has He accomplished by His death on the cross? What effect does His death on a cross have on us? With this book, we have selected key themes that focus on the Gospel with each character trait. However, to be clear, the following are the Gospel facts you should repeatedly review with your team members.

Gospel Facts:

The one and only one God, who is holy, made us in His image to know Him. However, we have sinned and cut ourselves off from Him. Because of God's love for us, God became a man in Jesus, lived a perfect life, and died on the cross. He fulfilled the law Himself by taking on the punishment we deserved for the sins of all those who ever turn to and trust Him. He rose again from the dead, showing that God accepted Christ's sacrifice and God's wrath against us had been exhausted. Now, God calls us to repent of our sins and trust in Christ. When we do, we are born again into a new life, an eternal life with God.

SPORTS WORLDVIEW ASSESSMENT

WHAT'S YOUR *Sports* WORLDVIEW?

In answering the set of questions you can determine the extent
to which your perspective aligns with Biblical values. The test
aims to shed light on how you can fortify your faith within sports.
Your responses will be kept completely confidential.

WorldView Quiz

WWW.KINGDOMSPORTS.ONLINE

KINGDOM
SPORTS

LOVE

GOD PURSUES ME

"Surely your goodness and unfailing love will pursue me all the days of my life and I will live in the house of the LORD forever." Psalm 23:6

On November 30, 1971, *"Brian's Song,"* starring James Caan and Billy Dee Williams, premiered on ABC. It was the most-watched made-for-TV movie in history. It's based on Chicago Bears Gale Sayers' account of his friendship with teammate Brian Piccolo. Piccolo and Sayers had very different temperaments. Racial backgrounds made them unlikely to become close friends in the 1960s. They became the first interracial roommates in NFL history. In the beginning, Piccolo helped Sayers return from a severe injury that could easily have ended his career. Later, Sayers returned the favor by helping his friend fight a losing battle to cancer. The most dramatic moment in the movie was Sayers' speech when he received the George Halas Most Courageous Player Trophy after successfully recovering from his knee injury. He said, "You flattered me by giving me this award, but I tell you here and now that I accept it for Brian Piccolo. Brian Piccolo is the man of courage who should receive the award. It is mine tonight—it is Brian Piccolo's tomorrow. I love Brian Piccolo, and I'd like all of you to love him, too. And tonight, when you hit your knees, please ask God to love him."

KingdomVideo

Love: Having a deep personal attachment and affection for another person.

1. Share a time when you were loved deeply. How did you feel?
2. Complete this sentence: I feel loved when _____.

Team Builder: Everyone spread out in an open area. When the leader yells "Everybody's it!" start running around trying to tag others while avoiding getting tagged. If you get tagged, sit down, extend your arms and try to tag those still running around. If two people tag each other at the same time, both must sit down. Play until one player is standing. Did you feel love during this game?

When Brittany Viola qualified for the 2012 Olympics, it was the culmination of a long journey complete with serious highs and lows. However, the platform diver says it was a serious battle with bulimia in 2006 that caused her to come face to face with her greatest struggle yet. While at an eating disorder facility in Arizona, Viola accepted Christ as her Savior, but once back at the University of Miami, she began to struggle again. That's when a teammate shared the truth of God's love with her and she was able to understand the power and truth found in these words written by David in Psalm 139:13-16.

Brittany shares, "There was light shining in times of darkness. As I continued to struggle with my eating disorder, I would be reminded God still loved me even when I did not love myself. His forgiveness helped me to forgive myself. His truth allowed me to replace the many lies in my head. He saw me as fearfully and wonderfully made, His perfect creation, chosen, holy, and dearly loved."

In Luke 19:1-10, we find a story of pursuit in a man named Zacchaeus. There was nothing special about Zacchaeus. In fact, he was despised by almost everyone who knew him. That's because Zacchaeus was a Jewish man working for the Roman Empire as a tax collector. At best, he was considered a loathsome cheat. At worst, he was viewed as a traitor against his own people.

However, when Jesus passed through his town, Zacchaeus wanted to catch a glimpse of the man everyone was talking about. He was described as a short man, so in order to see over the crowd, he climbed a tree for a better view. When Jesus came by, He looked up at Zacchaeus and said, "Quick, come down! I must be a guest in your home today" (v. 5).

Of all the people Jesus could have pursued, Zacchaeus was among the least likely candidates. The astonished people voiced their displeasure, and some even began to complain. "He has gone to be the guest of a notorious sinner," they grumbled (v. 7).

Zacchaeus was deeply moved by Jesus' unconditional love. He repented of sins right there and vowed to pay four times what he owed anyone he had cheated and give half of his wealth to the poor. Jesus responded by forgiving Zacchaeus of his sins and then spending time with him in his home.

WEIGHT TRAINING

1. Describe a dark time in your life. Did you feel God's love during that experience? Explain.

2. Why do you think Zacchaeus wanted to see Jesus so badly?

3. Why do you think Jesus' display of love had such a profound impact on Zacchaeus?

WRAP UP

God's amazing and relentless love changes lives and creates memorable stories.

1. Can you relate to any of these stories (Gale Sayers, Brian Piccolo, Brittany Viola or Zacchaeus)? How so? Take some time to share some of your story and how God's love has changed your life.

2. Do you ever struggle to embrace God's love for you? If so, why do you have a hard time believing it is true?

God's love has no limits and includes the following promises:

• **God's Love Is Unconditional.** God's love is not based on performance. Nothing will make God love you any less or any more than He already does. Read Isaiah 54:10.

• **God's Love Is For Everyone.** God doesn't love one person more than another. He loves you because you are His creation. Read Psalm 139:13-16.

• **God's Love Is Forever.** Because God is infinite, His love has no end. God's love is bottomless! Read 1 John 4:16. In John 15:13, the Bible says, "There is no greater love than to lay down one's life for one's friends."

3. How would these ancient statements from God's Word apply to your team dynamics? What are some things keeping you or your team from embracing God's love?

4. Do you think the more love there is on a team, the greater effort and teamwork, or is it more important for everyone to be tough? Why? How

might the Bible verses listed above help you overcome any doubts about God's love for you?

Any serious athlete has one goal in mind—to win the prize. The pursuit of the championship, trophy or medal drives the competitor to practice and play with intense focus and determination in order to obtain the ultimate reward. Passion drives them to reach the goal, but God too has a prize He is pursuing, and the prize is you. This is exactly why Jesus died on the cross in order to pay the penalty for our sin (John 3:16-17 and Romans 5:8).

God will never force you to accept His love. He offers it to you as a free gift and then allows you to make the choice—receive it or keep running from it. Until you choose to receive it, He will relentlessly pursue you and a real relationship with you.

If you want to discover God's love for you and know Jesus personally, turn to "The Four" beginning on page 100. If you have already made this life-changing commitment, ask God to reveal those areas in your life where you still need God's love to bring healing and understanding. Ask the Lord for guidance to help you as you begin your own pursuit of Him by prayerfully asking God to reveal His love to you. As you begin to receive and understand God's love, write down how His love changes you and how it will continue to impact you in the future.

COACHING CONNECTION

It feels good to be wanted. From the playground to the pros, top coaches and athletes are pursued to make the team better. Many times those pursuits are based on what we as individuals can do rather than who we are on the inside. Too often, once we have nothing else to offer or our talents and abilities are diminished, those who pursued us because of external qualities are suddenly less interested in continuing the relationship.

That's what makes God's love for us so remarkable. It's not based on our physical appearance, talents, how good a person we are or any good things we have done. The fact of the matter is we can never be good enough for God's love, yet as David wrote in Psalm 23:6, He pursues us all the days of our lives. It's true. More than anything, God wants a deep, meaningful love relationship with you!

BIG

GO BIG OR GO HOME

"Now all glory to God, who is able, through His mighty power at work within us, to accomplish infinitely more than we might ask or think." Ephesians 3:20

What does it mean to go big in everyday life? Where does the strength and power to do so come from? Why does it matter to give your all, in sports and in your faith?

KingdomVideo

"Go big or go home." This modern-day chant can be found throughout many aspects of society. The idea of making big statements to get big results is especially prevalent in the athletic world and with our career aspirations.

We were all born to dream, not just in our sleep at night or as we nod off during class. No, each of us has been given an innate desire to be something and to do something greater than our capabilities or our circumstances. Ephesians 3:20 is just one of many Scriptures affirming this truth. God is able to make the dreams He has given us come to pass.

Big: Possessing something of great significance.

1. What does it mean to go big in your sport or career?
2. What are some of the risks associated with going big? What are some of the rewards?

Team Builder: Go around the group and have each person share their biggest, craziest dream for their team or for their life. After each answer, respond to the following questions:

1. What would it take for your big dream to come true?
2. What are the obstacles keeping your big dream from coming to pass?

WARM-UP

Jim Caviezel went to the University of Washington as a walk-on to play basketball but was never able to compete as a varsity player. Yet, he could never shake the feeling God was calling him to an acting career. Upon graduation, he moved to Hollywood hoping to land a soap opera role. Boy did the Lord have bigger plans for Jim's career as evidenced by the number of major roles he has played on the big screen, including Jesus in *The Passion of the Christ* and Tim Ballard in *Sound of Freedom*.

When Jesus came to earth, it was to fulfill a big purpose to live a perfect, sinless life and to give up His life as a sacrifice so we could be restored back to God. To fulfill His purpose, Jesus found a group of regular, ordinary men to walk alongside Him. These 12 disciples didn't seem like they had much to offer. Most of them were fishermen. None of them were otherwise notable. Still, Jesus saw beyond their professions and human abilities. He saw great potential and huge opportunities for them to change the world. He chose to teach and train them so they could be part of His big mission. At first, they struggled believing He was the Son of God. To help them see the reality that Jesus was God, He showed them His power through a series of miracles: giving sight to the blind, making deaf ears hear, and causing the crippled to rise and walk. Even though they witnessed incredible miracles, the disciples still didn't fully understand how big and powerful Jesus was. They didn't know what to make of this man they called Teacher.

Everything changed one night as they all got into a boat and crossed the lake. Read Matthew 8:24-27. Even though the disciples had seen amazing miracles before, and even though they first-hand witnessed another miracle that saved their lives, the disciples still questioned Jesus' true identity. They saw His power and His unconditional love for each of them, and eventually they came to a full understanding of His divine nature as God.

We all have big hopes, big dreams, big goals, big ideas, and big aspirations, but we can only go so far on our own strength. We need a team we can rely on, and a Coach to lead us. If we are truly going to accomplish everything we've been born to achieve, it's going to require an active relationship with God—the Creator of the Universe and the Ultimate Coach—who is bigger and more powerful than anything!

WEIGHT TRAINING

1. Re-read Matthew 8:24-27. How do you think the disciples felt during the storm and when Jesus calmed it?

2. Based on their social standing and their backgrounds, do you think the disciples struggled to believe they were meant to fulfill a big purpose? Explain.

3. Do you ever struggle to believe God has a big purpose and plan for your life? How does His love for you help you with your disbelief? Explain.

WRAP UP

Here are three important truths from His Word about the bigness of God:

1. God's love is big. Not only did God create you in His image (Genesis 1:27), but even after mankind sinned against Him (Genesis 3:1-24), He set into motion a plan to redeem mankind back to Himself at a great cost—the life of His only Son (John 3:16). God continues to pursue us with His love no matter how far we try to run from Him, no matter how many mistakes we may have made. Read Romans 8:38.

2. God's power is big. There is no more powerful being than the creator of the universe. God transcends space and time and has always existed. He is so big that nothing in the galaxy or even the most microscopic cell misses His attention. Nothing is impossible for Him! Read Psalm 147:5.

3. God's purpose is big. He has a specific plan for your life. If you don't feel qualified, remember God qualifies the unqualified. God will equip you and empower you to fulfill the big purpose He has destined just for you. Read Jeremiah 29:11.

If you're ready to go big and start living out the destiny God has planned for you, do the following:

1. Believe in God's power. To start on this faith journey, you must first believe what Jesus said about Himself in the New Testament Gospels is true. Read John 14:6.

2. Receive God's power. Next, this journey requires faith on your part to accept the salvation He purchased for you by sacrificing Himself and dying on the cross. Read Ephesians 2:8-9. If you haven't yet made that commitment and would like to do so today, talk to one of your leaders. You can also learn more about salvation on pages 91-101.

3. Go in God's power. Surrender to His will and allow His power to work in your life. If you have already made this commitment, ask God to strengthen your faith in Him so you can actively trust Him as you pursue His purposes. Read Colossians 1:11.

Here are three big takeaways from this Workout:

- **Big God = Big Purpose.** There are no small, insignificant plans for those who follow God's heart.
- **Big God = Small Problems.** The obstacles of life might seem impossible to overcome, but God is bigger than any problem you might face.
- **Big God = Big Power.** If you don't feel like you can do what He has called you to do, God will equip you with His power. If you feel like your problems are too great, God will help you defeat them with that same power.

1. What are some ways you have personally felt God's love?
2. Have you experienced God's power in your life? Explain.
3. What do you think it means to have purpose and what do you believe is your purpose on this team? Do you believe you have what it takes to fulfill the purpose God has for you? Explain.
4. Read Matthew 28:18-20. Discuss the promise and the big plan God laid out for His disciples. What is your role in this plan?

COACHING CONNECTION

Just as the disciples needed to be reminded of just how big God truly was, we too need to experience His bigness through prayer, through the reading of His Word, and through His strength. Jesus is our source and His words in Matthew 28:18-20 are a powerful reminder of whom we serve and the big power to which we, as followers of Christ, have access.

Think about the areas of your life where you might be lacking a full understanding of God's love, power, and/or purpose. Ask God to give you a revelation of what it means to go big for Him and allow Him to be active in everything you do.

www.kingdomsports.online

BLESSING

INVOKING FAVOR AND HONOR

""Look, today I am giving you the choice between a blessing and a curse!"
Deuteronomy 11:26

If you love an amazing 'feel good' story and you are a sports fan, watch The Kendrick Brothers' *Show Me the Father* (2021) documentary film. It features the stories of Sherman Smith (retired NFL player and coach), Deland McCullough (NFL player/coach and current running backs coach at Notre Dame), Eddie George (1995 Heisman Trophy Winner and NFL running back), Dr. Tony Evans (NFL/NBA chaplain and pastor), Jim Daly (President, Focus on the Family) and others. The documentary underscores the undeniable fact that everyone has a unique father story. When talking to sons and daughters about their father, most people either claim their dad was a hero or a zero. If dad is present, they either love their dad deeply or they despise him. Whether positive or painful, it's always personal and can deeply affect the core of our identity and the direction of our lives. Providing a fresh perspective on the roles of fathers in today's society, the film not only invites you to think differently about how you view your own father but also how you personally relate to God.

Blessing: Invoking favor and honor upon another person.

1. On a scale of 0-10 (0–terrible and 10–excellent), rate your unique relationship with your dad and share why you gave him this number.
2. I believe many fathers wound their children unknowingly, and they certainly don't plan on it. If you were wounded, does your dad know your feelings? And if he does know, has this wound healed?

Team Builder: Watch *Show Me the Father* together. The documentary is exactly 90 minutes in length, so plan accordingly. After the movie ends, talk about what you saw and heard. Why is a father's blessing valuable and important?

Part of a pre-season football training camp on the high school, collegiate and professional level is determining who will be the starters for the first game. The quarterback battle typically gets the most attention from the entire team, coaches, fans and media. At some point prior to the kick-off, the head coach makes a decision and a blessing is given to the starting quarterback.

In Genesis 12:2, Abram (who later had his name changed to Abraham) is the recipient of a tremendous promise from God Almighty. God said, "I will make you into a great nation. I will bless you and make you famous, and you will be a blessing to others." From this point on, the transfer of a blessing from Abraham to the next generation and ultimately to future generations became very important to the future Israel nation. We see this vividly in the story of two twins, Esau and Jacob, born in Genesis 25. Esau, as the oldest twin of Isaac, was entitled to receive the blessing from his father Isaac, who had received his blessing from his father Abraham. Jacob, in a scheme worthy of a *Dateline* television drama, steals Esau's blessing. God's blessing upon Jacob, whose name is changed to Israel, later transfers the blessing to his children who eventually pass it on to their children's children.

The positive presence of a dad in a family shapes in many ways, a healthy masculinity in the lives of sons and also a healthy femininity in his daughters. On the flip side, the negative presence of a dad can create devastation. David Blankenhorn said, "As a father, the good family man is not perfect, but he is good enough to be irreplaceable. He is a father on the premises. He knows nothing can substitute for him. Nothing. He would never consider himself 'not that important' to his children. He is, in fact, essential."

It is a high calling and responsibility to be a dad. It has been said, "Any man can be a father, but it is a tremendous responsibility and honor to be a dad." Remember, all of us are flawed. No one is perfect. Dads are human, and they will mess up—some more than others. There's a very high percentage you have been wounded and deeply hurt by your dad.

Here's an indisputable fact we know about a dad. If a dad steps out of his home and shuns the responsibility of being a father, Satan steps into the void. The devil is eager and very willing to move into the home and fill the gap.

WEIGHT TRAINING

1. Do a Bible search on the word 'blessing.' What did you discover?

2. Bill Dotson, with Abiding Fathers, states that 90% of all men and women have a father wound. Have you ever heard of a father wound? Describe the ramifications of a person who has an unresolved father wound. Is there anyone on your team who would be willing to discuss how a father wound has impacted their life?

3. Why is a father's blessing important? Is there anyone on your team who would be willing to discuss how a father's blessing has impacted their life?

WRAP UP

Dads pass on a legacy to their family—one which is either godly or one of sin and wickedness. Fathers pass on God's blessing or God's curse to future generations. A dad who refuses to live a godly life passes on to his children a life of captivity. Often, according to Exodus 20:5, 34:7, Numbers 14:18, Deuteronomy 5:9 and numerous other passages, a dad's sin is reproduced and the sin extends to the third and fourth generations. There is a direct tie between generational bondage and generational sin, which is why you find certain sins wreaking havoc on a family line generation after generation.

Second Chronicles 26-28 details the progression of generational sin which began with King Uzziah. Pastor Phil Hopper summarizes it this way, "What began in the first generation (Uzziah) of failing to take God seriously and obeying God completely was reproduced in the second generation (Jotham) with spiritual apathy and compromise with idolatry. It was then reproduced in the third generation (Ahaz) with a complete rejection of God and full-blown idolatry. It ends with the fourth generation with a number of Ahaz's children being sacrificed in the fires of a foreign God—Molech." Perhaps if Uzziah had realized his disobedience many years earlier was going to result in his great grandchildren's awful deaths, he might have chosen to live a godly, holy life and passed along a blessing instead.

Ahaz's son, Hezekiah, broke the generational curse and within the first 30 days of being king, he announced there was a new sheriff in town. He purged the nation of the ways of his father by destroying the false idols. He pledged his allegiance to God Almighty. He invited the people to repent and join him in serving God. The tribe of Judah responded to his leadership, and the blessing of God came upon all the land under King Hezekiah's leadership.

According to Dr. John Trent (Stronger Families) there are five elements to giving a powerful blessing:
1. Give a meaningful touch and joyful face.
2. Give a spoken message, specific to the person you are honoring.
3. Attach high value to them by speaking of their character and strengths.
4. Speak of a special future, where they are going. God has plans for them, to bless them and use them in a powerful way.
5. Make a commitment to honor and support them always.

In Scripture, a blessing is given in Numbers 6:22-27 and Deuteronomy 30:15-20. God gives the people a choice between life and death, blessings and curses. To bless means to value and offer respect to another person. To curse means to cut off and dam up. Life is movement, and death is stagnation.

1. What does Scripture say about generational sin and the need for a blessing?
2. Read Proverbs 20:7. As a son or daughter, did you get what you needed from your dad and mom growing up? If not, what did you miss? Is it possible to reclaim some of what you missed now?
3. If you have been wounded by one or both of your parents, how has this wound impacted your life?
4. Have you ever received a blessing? If so, describe what happened? If not, would you like one and who would be the right person to give you this blessing?

COACHING CONNECTION

According to Jesus, with God's help, we can even bless those who curse us. Healing can go backward. To forgive means to untie the binding knots. This is the same word Jesus used when he said to unbind Lazarus and let him go. When the enemy wants to rob us of our purpose, we can help others see and reconnect with their purpose. We are challenged to give a blessing and to be a blessing!

Are there players on your team who need to be blessed? Would you consider helping facilitate this blessing or perhaps even being the one who does so? When you bless a person, include the words—I love you, I believe in you, I am for you and I trust you!!

BREADTH

HEART ISSUES

"Guard your heart above all else, for it determines the course of your life."
Proverbs 4:23

C arl 'Sugarfoot' Joseph's story is the stuff of which legends are made. His indomitable spirit has provided inspiration and hope across the globe. His story has been featured on numerous television shows. He was named the 1981 Most Courageous Athlete by the Philadelphia Sports Writers Association, and is the subject of a biography *"One of a Kind: The Legend of Carl Joseph."*

KingdomVideo

Carl Joseph was born without his left leg, but this didn't stop him from earning 13 varsity letters in football, basketball and track in the late 1970s and early 1980s at Florida's Madison High. Joseph started two years at nose guard and captained the football squad his senior year, cleared 5-10 in the high jump and dunked a basketball. He had personal bests of over 40' in the shot put and 130' in the discus throw. He did all of this by hopping on a right leg that was almost as wide as his waist. He didn't wear an artificial limb because they were not allowed in competition. People who watched him said he looked like a 'bewitched jackhammer' on the field. In spite of his obvious disability, Joseph showed the character quality of 'breadth' by displaying an amazing heart.

Breadth: Having depth and broadness, in words and deeds, within the heart and mind.

1. Identify someone who has inspired you because of his or her ability to overcome great obstacles. Why is this person an inspiration?
2. What role does the heart play in competitive sports? Name someone on your team who displays breadth. Why did you select this person?

Team Builder: Go to YouTube and search for Carl Joseph. See for yourself this man who has incredible depth and breadth in the way he lives his life. What are some of the life principles you can learn from him?

After high school, Carl Joseph was invited by Jackie Sherill, then head football coach for the University of Pittsburgh, to become manager of the football team during the 1980-81 school year. Afterward, Joseph returned to Florida and played linebacker and lineman for Bethune-Cookman College. Joseph became known for his special-teams play at Bethune-Cookman. "The impact on all our kids and on how they perform is something," Coach Bobby Frazier once stated. "When it's rough and Carl's in there, we know we can do it. I'd love to see what he'd do with all his limbs." The inspiring story of Carl Joseph was celebrated in 2009 when he was inducted into the Florida High School Athletic Hall of Fame in Gainesville.

"It's an accomplishment beyond my wildest imagination," Joseph said. "To see a one-legged guy be blessed to become part of a Hall of Fame with elite athletes like Emmitt Smith and Cris Collinsworth, it's a wonderful honor." Joseph served as senior bishop at Tallahassee's Holy Jerusalem Church of God. He has had health problems and no longer plays sports, although he coached high school football for 15 years. He gets around these days on crutches. "I've always said that I never thought of myself as handicapped," he said. "It was never talked about in my household, so I always considered myself an average kid. I always felt I could do with one leg what kids did with two legs." He said, "My mama never felt sorry for me, and I never felt sorry for myself. Believe you can do it, and Christ can do the rest."

Carl's story reminds me of 2 Corinthians 4:8-9, where in spite of the obstacles Paul faced, he would not be defeated. It reads, "We are pressed on every side by troubles, but we are not crushed. We are perplexed but not driven to despair. We are hunted down but never abandoned by God. We get knocked down, but we are not destroyed." To have breadth means you have something very special deep in your heart and soul allowing you to push beyond human capabilities.

Charles Jefferson also described Jesus Christ in the same way, "In Jesus of Nazareth we get a revelation of the breadth of the heart of the Eternal. How did it happen Jesus was so spacious in His ideas, so broad in His sympathies and so far-reaching in His plans? It was because God was in Him revealing Himself to men. That is what God always is—broad in His sympathies, wonderful in His expectations, boundless in His love. *He so loved the world that He gave His only begotten Son.*"

WEIGHT TRAINING

1. Jerry Bridges said, "The word heart in Scripture is used in various ways. Sometimes it means our reason or understanding, sometimes our affections and emotions, and sometimes our will. Generally it denotes the whole soul of a man and all its faculties, not individually, but as they work together in doing good or evil. The MIND as it reasons, discerns and judges; the EMOTIONS as they like or dislike; the CONSCIENCE as it determines and warns and the WILL as it chooses or refuses—are all together called the heart." Discuss the four different components of the heart and the role each plays in your success, individually and as a team.

2. In your own words, describe the connection between the heart and love.

WRAP UP

In this Workout, let's focus on the heart. One translation of Proverbs 4:23 says, "Above all else guard your heart, for from it flows the wellsprings of life." Another translation says it this way, "From your heart flows everything." Many coaches will tell you an athlete with heart can many times contribute far above the one who has natural abilities. The heart is what God cares about most.

According to John Eldridge, the subject of the heart is addressed in the Bible more than any other topic—more than works or service, more than belief or obedience, more than money, and even more than worship. Proverbs 21:2 says, "People may be right in their own eyes, but the LORD examines their heart." Eldridge states, "By taking out your heart, the enemy takes you out." This is why guarding your heart is critical for every believer.

There is no escaping the centrality of the heart. God knows this truth, and it's why He made it the central theme of the Bible, just as He placed the physical heart in the center of the human body. Our deepest thoughts are found in the heart. The heart is the source of all creativity, courage, conviction and faith, hope and love. It is the essence of our existence and the center of our being. Romans 10:9-10 says saving faith only happens when we believe in our heart. You are not a Christian until you engage your heart—fully believing in Him with your heart.

Here are six keys to having a complete heart:

1. A desire to know God (Key Word: Relationship) – Psalm 37:4
2. A heart seeking after Him (Key Word: Pursuit) – Psalm 119:10 and 9:1
3. Totally trusting God (Key Word: Belief) – Proverbs 3:5-6
4. A desire to please God (Key Word: Ambition) – 2 Corinthians 5:9
5. Brokenness before God (Key Word: Humility) – Psalm 51:17
6. Responsiveness to people (Key Word: Servant) – 2 Corinthians 4:16-18

The heart is the connection point between you and God. This goes way beyond principles, duties and programs. It is not activities or information that change the way we live. The transformation and then the relationship each take place in the heart. One of the great verses of Scripture states, "If you look for Me wholeheartedly, you will find Me" (Jeremiah 29:13).

It has been said, "God isn't looking for perfection, He's looking for direction." If perfection was the standard, none of us would have a chance with God. Therefore, have a heart fully devoted to Christ and head in the right direction.

1. Read the verses above on "Six Keys to a Complete Heart" and comment on each statement and keyword identified. What are the results of having a complete heart? Did you notice there is an increasing depth of love as you move from the first key to the last one?
2. Why does God care about our heart so much?
3. Do a heart check with your team as individuals and as a group. Are you fully engaged with your heart or are you just going through the motions? How can you tell the difference?

COACHING CONNECTION

There were over 40 Old Testament kings who ruled over Judah and Israel spanning hundreds of years. A large majority of the kings didn't have a heart for God and His Word, but a few, including David, Asa, Jehoshaphat, Josiah, and Hezekiah, had the type of heart which pleased God. King David wasn't a perfect man, but God said David, not Saul, was a man who had the type of heart He was looking for based on 1 Samuel 16:7 which reads, "But the LORD said to Samuel, "Don't judge by his appearance or height, for I have rejected him. The LORD doesn't see things the way you see them. People judge by outward appearance, but the LORD looks at the heart." Acts 13:22 confirms David's heart, "But God removed Saul and replaced him with David...He will do everything I want him to do."

FAMILY

BETTER TOGETHER

"...so it is with Christ's body. We are many parts of one body, and we all belong to each other." Romans 12:5

F amily. For some, the word 'family' conjures positive images from home or brings to mind valued relation-ships in a shared setting. For others, the thought of family might stir up sadness or even painful memories. I was fortunate to grow up in a Christian home with parents who prioritized church and being in God's Word. I learned at an early age of God's love for me. My church friends became extended family members. Even with this great foundation, every family has dysfunc-tion, and ours had issues. There were times when our family was fractured. It was hard to love. Obviously, being an athlete is hard. Being a follower of Christ is even harder. There's no way you can do either of those things successfully on your own. You have to be 'family strong' if you want to get through any ad-versity and if you want to fulfill your God-given purpose. This means you must have people around you who will encourage you, build you up, work toward the same goals, and be there for you when times get tough.

KingdomVideo

Family: Being part of something bigger than yourself.

1. What do you think of when you hear the word 'family?'
2. What are some things that bond a team like family?

Team Builder: Divide the group into circles of 10-12 people, each facing in-ward. Everyone then reaches across with one arm and grabs someone else's hand, interweaving hands and arm in a random fashion. Do the same for the other hand. Now try to get everyone back into a perfect circle while still hold-ing hands. Letting go is not an option. It takes communication, cooperation and a sense of humor. What aspects of family and team come to mind after playing this 'human knot' game? How is your team like a family?

WARM-UP

In 1979, the Pittsburgh Pirates captured the imagination of baseball fans in their home city and across the country with a colorful cast of characters that included All-Stars Willie Stargell, Dave Parker, and Kent Tekulve. The team even had a theme song called "We Are Family" played throughout the season and all the way to a World Series championship. The concepts of sports and family became intertwined.

During His ministry on earth, Jesus became known for performing amazing miracles. He gave sight to the blind, gave hearing to the deaf, made the lame to walk again, and even brought the dead back to life. His reputation spread throughout Judea and oftentimes people needing help would seek Him out.

This was the case with four men who heard Jesus was teaching in a nearby home. In this story (Mark 2:1-12), the men had a friend who was paralyzed and believed Jesus could heal him. They placed him on a mat and carried him to the house, but it was too crowded and there was no room inside.

The friends were determined to help their friend. They worked together to lift him onto the roof, where they opened a hole and lowered him down on the mat directly in front of Jesus who saw his friends' faith and forgave the man's sins (v. 5). Then, after rebuking the religious leaders who doubted Jesus had the authority to do such a thing, Jesus turned back to the man, "Stand up, pick up your mat, and go home" (v. 11).

The man "jumped up, grabbed his mat, and walked out through the stunned onlookers" (v. 12), but the miracle would have never happened if those four men hadn't worked together as a team to get their friend to Jesus.

In your family and on your team, you are individually made better when you are working together with others. In fact, most situations in sports and in life require teamwork in order for any significant accomplishments to be achieved. It's especially true when it comes to growing in your relationship with Jesus.

In sports and in life, family is an essential component to success and a vital key to dealing with adversity and failure. You need a team, a group of Christians, to come alongside you to encourage you, guide you and support you in your faith journey.

WEIGHT TRAINING

1. What are some words describing the men from Mark 2:1-12 who worked together to help their friend get to Jesus?

2. Share a time when you worked together with your family or your team-mates to accomplish an important task.

3. What happens when even just one person doesn't show up or worse yet, refuses to fulfill their role on the team?

4. Do a Bible search creating a list of all the 'one another's' cited. After completing, how can you lead with love on a daily basis?

WRAP UP

For a family or team to be physically, emotionally and spiritually successful, there are three key biblical principles.

1. Jesus Wants Your Family and Team To Be Strong. In sports and in life, a strong team is vital to fulfilling the call He has for your life. A family member or teammate's job is to encourage and build up those around them. A true family always has your back. They are also responsible for holding others account-able and letting them know when they are getting off track or making poor decisions. Read Proverbs 27:17.

2. Jesus Wants Your Family and Team To Bless Others. Strong families and teams aren't meant to serve selfish interests but rather to make others better and encourage those around them. If a team is going to be successful, its indi-vidual members must have the same mindset, the same goals, and the same worldview. In other words, families are unified. For the spiritual family, this means tapping into the unifying power only Jesus can give. Read Matthew 18:20.

3. Jesus Wants To Lead Your Family and Team By Creating Community. The biggest purpose behind a family or a team isn't to achieve material success but rather to be a blessing and make others better. Each member has a specif-ic function that makes the larger unit work effectively toward a goal. A family or team will only go as far as their leader can take them. There's no greater leader to follow than Jesus—the greatest leader to ever walk the earth. Read Romans 12:4-5.

Perhaps your family is found within your home. Maybe you consider your sports team to be your family, or you might look to a group of friends to fill that role in your life. Take a few minutes to write down who you consider your family (e.g. father/mother, sister/brother, other relatives, teammates, friends, etc.) and the role they play in your life (e.g. encourager, protector, coach, mentor, etc.).

Look closely at the family roster you created. First of all, thank God for the people on your list and what they represent to you. Then, ask the Lord to send other people to fill in any blank spots on your list—parents, friends, teammates, coaches, teachers, mentors, etc., who will come alongside and help you grow in your relationship with God.

1. Describe some of the important members of your family or team.
2. What are some positions that need to be filled on your family or team? Go back and fill in some of those positions and describe their role even if you don't have a 'player' name to fill in on the team.
3. How do you think filling those roles might make your family or team stronger?
4. God desires you to be part of His family. What are the benefits of being part of God's family that provides love and acceptance?

COACHING CONNECTION

Within any strong family or team, the motivator for every action must be love—not just emotional, feel-good love, but unconditional action-oriented love that digs deep into the heart. Jesus made this clear to His followers as noted in John 13:34-35, "So now I am giving you a new commandment: Love each other. Just as I have loved you, you should love each other. Your love for one another will prove to the world that you are My disciples."

What do you do if you don't have a strong Christian family, team or support system? Get plugged in. Go find a church. Go find an FCA Huddle in your community. Be proactive and seek out like-minded people who will lock arms with you and help you learn how to live like Him and live for Him. Read Hebrews 10:24-25.

FEAR

LOVE OVERCOMES FEAR

"Such love has no fear, because perfect love expels all fear. If we are afraid, it is for fear of punishment, and this shows that we have not fully experienced His perfect love. We love each other because He loved us first." 1 John 4:18-19

Some opponents are greater challenges than others. We may enter one contest with great self-assurance while another match-up might cause concern. For all athletes, coaches and teams, however, there is likely no more dominant competitor than fear. We can deny it all we want, but we all fear something—failure, losing, getting cut, injuries, rejection, etc. Fear can cause us to play timidly, make mistakes, quit before the task has been completed, or mentally and physically shut down. Fear doesn't stop there. Fear also creeps into other aspects of life. It keeps us from doing important things like living for Jesus, serving others, speaking out against injustice, and fulfilling God's call.

KingdomVideo

Fear: Having unpleasant emotions brought on by dangerous, painful or threatening situations.

1. What are some common fears you have (spiders, snakes, heights, deep water, tight spaces, public speaking, etc.)? What is one of your fears most people might not know about?
2. What fears are currently holding you back?

Team Builder: Test your fears based on these questions: Would you rather skydive from 10,000 feet or scuba dive 1,000 feet into the ocean? Would you rather hold a tarantula or a python? Would you rather give a speech in front of the President or sing in front of an award-winning recording artist? Would you rather be stuck in an elevator or a small cave? Would you rather rappel from the Empire State Building or climb Mount Everest? What did you learn about yourself and your teammates from these fear-based questions?

Charlotte Brown was born with normal vision, but problems with her sight arose as an infant and continued to worsen into grade school. After multiple surgeries, she was declared legally blind. Brown can't distinguish shapes and has no depth perception. Yet this didn't stop the Texas high school athlete from competing and qualifying for the state track and field meet in the challenging pole vault event. With a few technological aids and vocal cues from her coach, Brown managed to do what many thought to be impossible, but above all, she credits her parents' love for helping her conquer any fears. "My family has always encouraged me," she said. "They never said, 'you can't.'"

Jimmy Morris had a similar experience when he made an inspirational comeback and earned a spot on the Tampa Bay Rays roster after 10 years away from baseball. Injuries took him away from the game, but his love for the high school players he was coaching at the time and the support of his wife gave him the courage to pitch again. Morris' story was later famously told in the popular movie *The Rookie*.

During the 1992 Summer Olympics in Barcelona, there was an emotional moment when medal favorite Derek Redmond from England tore his hamstring during the 400-meter semi-final. While struggling to finish the race, his father, Jim, broke through security and ran onto the track. The sight of a father helping his son hobble to the finish line is still one of the Olympics' most enduring images.

Although there are many differences in these three stories, there is one major similarity. All of these athletes relied on loving relationships with others to overcome their fears and achieve great things.

According to 1 John 4:18-19, a person who lives in fear doesn't fully believe God's love story. The word 'perfect' (v. 18) references completeness. It means you have a mature understanding of God's complete love which is incompatible with fear. Literally, fear has been expelled from your heart. The 'fear of punishment' carries an eternal torment pointing out an unloving believer's guilt and fear to meet a Holy God. Such fear prohibits a completed love. In contrast, a true loving believer of Christ has nothing to fear and thus escapes the inner torment which a failure to love can bring. The result of perfect love is found in verse 19. Therefore, there is no fear in the life of a believer because his love for God originates in God's love for him.

WEIGHT TRAINING

1. Do any of these fears apply to you? Failure, death, making a mistake, rejection, physical harm, the future, God's judgment, being alone, ridicule. Take some time to share one of your fears with your teammates and how those fears have kept you from discovering and fulfilling God's purpose for your life.

2. Re-read and discuss the ramifications of 1 John 4:18-19. How could understanding God's love for us begin to drive fear out of your life?

3. Can you describe a time when a teammate's love for you gave you courage? If so, share with the team.

WRAP UP

Fear of all types is something God knew humans would battle daily. Did you know the most cited statement uttered by God occurs 365 times in Scripture? It is these powerful words, "Do not be afraid." Coincidence? I think not.

In Luke 15:11-32, Jesus tells a story about a rich man and his two sons. The younger son was restless and wanted to explore life outside his home. So he asked his father to give him his inheritance before the time had come. The young man traveled to a distant country and quickly squandered his wealth. When a famine overtook the land, he had nothing and the only work he could find was feeding pigs. He was so hungry even the pig slop looked good to him. That's when he came to his senses and returned to his father, where he feared rejection but hoped he might at least become a hired hand. As the young man approached his father's estate, the fear quickly melted away because, from a distance, his father had been watching and waiting for him to return. The father ran to his son, embraced him and greeted him with a kiss. Instead of condemning his son he forgave him, loved him, and threw a party in his honor.

While the story of the Prodigal Son serves as a metaphor of God's love for us, Jesus demonstrated the same love in a very real and tangible way. Just before He was betrayed by His disciple Judas and taken away by the Roman soldiers, Jesus went with the other disciples to a garden called Gethsemane and asked them to pray with Him through the night. While His friends slept, Jesus prayed with such intensity that His sweat became like drops of blood (Luke 22:44). His flesh was gripped with fear over the brutal torture and death His body was about to endure for our sins, but each time He prayed, He surrendered to God's plan because of His great love for us.

Here are a few key points related to the truth about fear:

• **Fear is strong.** Fear can grip our hearts and stop us from having a personal relationship with God who loves us more than we can think or even imagine. Further, even in the life of a believer, it can stall us from pursuing God's plan for our lives. Fear often paralyzes us from accomplishing our goals, inhibiting our untapped potential. Read Ephesians 3:20-21.

• **God's love is stronger.** God's love always overcomes fear. Once we fully embrace God's love, fear's stronghold is broken and no longer has a place in our lives. We can then achieve whatever dreams He has placed in our hearts. Read Deuteronomy 31:6; Joshua 1:9 and Isaiah 41:10.

1. Have you ever been fearful after making a mistake or a bad decision like the young man in Luke 15? Explain.
2. What does the story of Jesus in the garden speak to your heart about how much He loves you?
3. Can you think of a time when fear kept you from doing something you knew you were supposed to do? If so, share with your teammates how you felt about letting fear control you.
4. Read Psalm 56:3-4. Why is the defeat of fear so important when it comes to fulfilling God's purpose?

COACHING CONNECTION

Here's a well-known acronym for FEAR—False Evidence Appearing Real. It is estimated by researchers that more than 90% of the things we fear never happen. How have your fears stopped you from experiencing a full and abundant life?

Without divine love, Jesus would not have made it to the cross. As Jesus displayed His perfect love for us, He demonstrated what it looks like to overcome fear and gave us the example we can use whenever fear seeks to shut us down. There is, in fact, no fear we cannot defeat if we understand the inspired truth the Apostle Paul shared with the Christians in Romans 8:38-39. When we wholeheartedly believe this verse is true, we can take another step toward experiencing the promises of God.

FORGIVENESS

HAPPINESS = FORGIVING EASILY

"But when you are praying, first forgive anyone you are holding a grudge against, so that your Father in heaven will forgive your sins, too." Mark 11:25

The 'Fab Five,' the 1991-92 University of Michigan men's basketball team, was the first team in NCAA history to compete in the championship game with all-freshman starters. The 'Fab Five' returned to the 1993 title game as sophomores in a game remembered for Chris Webber's costly timeout. With 11 seconds remaining and his team down by two points Webber signaled for a timeout, but his team had none left. This resulted in a technical foul securing North Carolina's victory.

KingdomVideo

In every game, mistakes are made—errant throws, dropped balls, strikeouts, or falling down at inopportune moments. Few mistakes are as costly as Webber's, but many professionals blow it during televised games for the whole world to see. Are these athletes not allowed to play anymore? Not at all. In fact, the player who made the mistake is often immediately relied on by his teammates to do it right on the next possession.

Forgiveness: Clearing the record of those who have wronged me and not holding their past offenses against them.

1.   Have you ever blown it in a game? How did your teammates react? The fans? How did their reactions make you feel?
2.   What advice would you give a teammate if he/she made a critical mistake at the end of a game costing your team a win?

Team Builder: Ask each person to find a partner and share his or her most humiliating moment in sports (dropping a pass, shooting a game-losing airball, whiffing on a volleyball spike, etc.). What bearing did it have upon the game? Have a few people share their stories with the entire group.

WARM-UP

My good friend Barney Sarver faithfully served on the FCA staff in the state of Texas for 39 years. Late in his FCA career, his beloved wife was killed in a tragic car accident involving a 17-year-old drunk driver. Rather than pressing charges, Barney asked the judge for leniency and the opportunity for her killer to serve his community service hours under Barney's supervision. Barney's forgiveness resulted in this young man accepting Christ.

All of us have been hurt by strangers or someone we deeply care about. These hurts can leave us angry and bitter. God's solution? Read Ephesians 4:31-32. If we are going to experience God fully, we must choose to forgive.

A number of studies reveal it is not great wealth that makes people happy, but having friends and forgiveness. Commenting on these findings in a *USA Today* article, Marilyn Elias says, "The happiest people surround themselves with family and friends, don't care about keeping up with the Joneses next door, lose themselves in daily activities, and most important, forgive easily."

An unforgiving spirit is often the last emotional fortress we yield to God. Even as Christians, we often cling to anger and bitterness, feeling those who have wronged us should suffer for their offenses. However, when we realize how much God has forgiven us, it compels us to extend mercy (Colossians 3:12-13). Forgiving others is God's command to us and promises a life full of love, peace, thankfulness, and joy. Freely we have been forgiven; let us freely forgive. Someone said, "Forgiveness is agreeing to live with the consequences of another person's sin. Forgiveness is costly; we pay the price of the evil we forgive. Yet you're going to live with those consequences whether you want to or not; your only choice is whether you will do so in the bondage of bitterness or the freedom of forgiveness. That's how Jesus forgave you—He took the consequences of your sin upon Himself. All true forgiveness is substitutional because no one really forgives without bearing the penalty of the other person's sin."

The forgiveness God gives is genuinely 'Good News.' We have all made mistakes we regret, but many of us have seen blame and denial modeled as responses to sin, and these only produce more sinful behavior. God is the God of second, third, fourth chances...and on and on. Read Psalm 86:5. The forgiveness of God washes us clean.

WEIGHT TRAINING

1. Think of a situation outside of sports when you've made an obvious mistake. How did you feel? How did others around you react? How do you think Jesus reacted to your mistake?

2. Respond to this quote. "When it seems you can't forgive, remember how much you've been forgiven." Discuss the forgiveness you have been extended by Jesus Christ. How does this impact you?

3. Do you forgive others easily? Why or why not?

WRAP UP

Why then do we forgive? Because Christ forgave us. God the Father "made Him who knew no sin to be sin on our behalf, that we might become the righteousness of God in Him" (2 Corinthians 5:21). Where is the justice? The cross makes forgiveness legally and morally right: "When He died, He died once to break the power of sin..." (Romans 6:10).

The sobering words of Matthew 6:14-15 underscore why we forgive. As an example, read the parable of the unmerciful servant in Matthew 18:21-35, who was delivered from a multi-million-dollar debt in today's dollars. After his release, the servant sought restitution from someone who owed him a much smaller amount (less than $20). The servant's story doesn't end well.

So how do you forgive from the heart? First, you must acknowledge the hurt and hate—the emotional core of your soul. Simply brushing aside the pain is something many Christians mistakenly believe they should do because they are Christians, but that's a cover-up. We need to let God bring the pain to the surface so He can deal with it. Then healing can begin.

Secondly, ask God to bring to your mind those you need to forgive. Make a list of all who have offended you. Since God has forgiven them by His grace, you can forgive them too. For each person on your list, say: "Lord, I forgive (name) for (offenses)." Keep praying about each individual until you are sure all the remembered pain has been dealt with. Don't try to rationalize or explain the offender's behavior. Forgiveness deals with your pain, not another's behavior. Remember, positive feelings will follow in time; freeing yourself from the pain of the past is the critical issue.

Forgiving is tough. Letting go of past wrongs, deep resentments, or personal betrayals can seem impossible. However, counselors, psychologists and even medical doctors have seen miracles occur because of the healing power of forgiveness. It is often a crucial component of emotional recovery, family reconciliation, and in some cases, improved physical health.

1. Peter blew it when he denied Jesus three times just prior to His crucifixion. Read the entire story in Luke 22:54-62 and Matthew 26:57-75 and answer the following questions:
    - Why did Peter deny Jesus three times?
    - What impact did this have on Peter and on Jesus?
    - What ultimately resulted following Peter's major mistake?
2. Share a time you were extended forgiveness and how it felt to be forgiven.
3. Is there a current situation on your team, at school or at work where forgiveness is needed? If so, make plans right now to get this situation resolved by asking someone to help you follow through with your commitment to forgive.
4. Is there anyone you need to personally forgive? I encourage you to take the first step toward reconciliation.

COACHING CONNECTION

We serve an amazing God who has freely extended His forgiveness to us through the shed blood of Jesus Christ. We have been forgiven a debt we could never repay. With your debt fully forgiven by Christ, you are now challenged to forgive others as well. When you choose to forgive, you release them by turning the person and the situation over to God. It is releasing the anger and the responsibility for judging them to the Lord. Just as you ask Jesus to "forgive us our debts" each day, you must ask Him to help you "forgive our debtors."

Throughout this whole workout is there someone the Lord placed on your mind who needs to receive forgiveness from you? While it may be awkward, I urge you not to delay this very important conversation.

HATE

LOVE OBLITERATES HATE

"There are six things the LORD hates—no, seven things He detests: haughty eyes, a lying tongue, hands that kill the innocent, a heart that plots evil, feet that race to do wrong, a false witness who pours out lies, a person who sows discord in a family." Proverbs 6:16-19

The NFL, NFLPA and the Minnesota Vikings issued a statement in September 2023 condemning the online hate speech directed at Minnesota running back Alexander Mattison after a loss in Philadelphia. Mattison shared some revolting and vulgar messages sent to him on Instagram, which included racial slurs and a suggestion he take his own life. Mattison responded in part, "This is not okay. Ya'll can come after me about fantasy (football) and blah blah blah...but this is unacceptable. Under my helmet I'm a human, a father, a son. This is sick."

KingdomVideo

The Vikings responded forcefully. "We are sickened by the hatred and racial slurs directed at Mattison following last night's game. There is simply no room for racist words or actions in sports or society. The Vikings will continue to fight to eliminate hate, to educate and to foster a diverse, equitable and inclusive community that respects and values our unique backgrounds. We will stand with Alexander and all players who, unfortunately, experience this type of ignorant and prejudicial behavior, and we ask our fans to continue to fight to eliminate racism." The league offered a similar rebuke.

Hate: An intense and passionate dislike for someone or something.

1. Without naming individuals, what are some things you hate?
2. Is hate, in and of itself, sinful? Why or why not?

Team Builder: Do a Bible search on the word 'hate' and create two lists. The first list includes things the Bible says we are to hate, and the second are the things we are not supposed to hate. What did you learn based on what the Bible says about hate?

Clearly, the Bible addresses the issue of hate, and one thing you'll notice is our hate is not to be directed at individuals, such as Alexander Mattison, but on the actions of those who are doing the hating. For example, Malachi 2:16 says, "'For I hate divorce!' says the LORD, the God of Israel. 'To divorce your wife is to overwhelm her with cruelty,' says the LORD of Heaven's Armies. 'So guard your heart; do not be unfaithful to your wife.'" Notice here the Lord says He hates divorce, but He is not saying He hates people who get divorced. It has been said, "God hates the sin but loves the sinner."

Another example of clarifying hate is seen in Luke 14:26. The key word in this verse is the word 'comparison.' Here Jesus emphasizes discipleship is difficult, so He suggests one must hate his own family and even his own life in order to be His disciple. Yet, hating one's family would have been a major violation of the Law. Since Jesus on multiple occasions admonished others to fulfill the Law, He did not mean one should literally hate his family. The emphasis here is on the priority of love. One's loyalty to Jesus must come before loyalty to family or even to life itself. Indeed, those who followed Jesus against their families' desires were probably thought of as hating their families.

Jesus even turns the subject of hate upside down in Luke 6:27. He uses this verse as a launching pad to mention seven aspects of unconditional love (Luke 6:27-31). These actions, not committed naturally by human effort, require supernatural enabling and thus are proof of true righteousness: (1) Love your enemies. (2) Do good to those who hate you. (3) Bless those who curse you. (4) Pray for those who mistreat you. (5) Do not retaliate. (6) Give freely. (7) Treat others the way you want to be treated.

This kind of love defines genuine Christianity and mirrors the same characteristics of our Heavenly Father. Jesus goes on to teach His followers a fundamental principle of the universe—what one sows he will reap (Luke 6:36-38 and Galatians 6:7). Jesus outlined five areas which were proof of the sowing and reaping theme, mentioned so often in Scripture: (1) Mercy will lead to mercy. (2) Judgment will lead to judgment. (3) Condemnation will lead to condemnation. (4) Pardon will lead to pardon. (5) Giving will lead to giving. It is simply a fact of life that certain attitudes and actions often reflect back on the individual. Read 1 John 4:7-21 and 1 Peter 1:22. Obliterate hate and instead choose love.

WEIGHT TRAINING

1. Re-read all passages referenced so far in this Workout. Have your views on hate changed based on what God says about it? If so, how?

2. What does it mean 'to hate the sin but love the sinner?' How is this even possible?

3. Have you experienced hatred firsthand? What role did love play in de-escalating or even eliminating the hate?

4. Without naming the person, are you hating on someone right now? What can you do to see this person in a loving way?

WRAP UP

Hatred and negativity kills people. Proverbs 18:1 points out, "The tongue can bring death or life..." To illustrate this fact, consider what happened to American soldiers detained in the Korean War. These POWs experienced the most extreme and effective hatred methods ever inflicted on record—resulting in death and devastation. The soldiers were detained in camps not considered especially cruel or unusual by conventional standards. They had adequate food, water and shelter, and they weren't subjected to common physical torture techniques such as having bamboo shoots driven under their fingernails. In fact, physical abuse in the North Korean POW camps was virtually non-existent.

However, despite minimal physical torture, the death rate was an incredible 38%, the highest POW death rate in U.S. military history and three times above the normal. Why, then, did so many American soldiers die? They weren't hemmed in with barbed wire; armed guards didn't surround the camps, yet no soldier ever tried to escape. Furthermore, these men regularly broke rank and turned against each other, sometimes forming close relationships with their captors. Astonishingly more than half the soldiers died simply because they had given up. The hatred inflicted upon them consumed them mentally.

The North Koreans' objective was to "deny men the emotional support coming from interpersonal relationships." The captors used four hate tactics:

1. **Informing.** Rewards such as cigarettes were given out when they snitched on one another. The intent was to break relationships and turn the men against each other.
2. **Self-criticism.** Every day they were gathered in small groups of 10-12 soldiers, and were required to confess all the bad things they had done, as well as all the good things they could have done but failed to do.
3. **Breaking loyalty to leadership and country.** They were constantly reminded of how everyone hated them by evidence of being abandoned in this hell hole.
4. **Withholding all positive emotional support.** All supportive letters received from home were withheld. All negative letters, however, such as a relative passing or a wife wanting a divorce, were immediately delivered.

A new killer disease resulted in the POW camps—extreme hopelessness. Soldiers would wander into their hut with the mindset there was no use in trying to survive. He would crawl into bed, pull a blanket over his head and die within two days. The soldiers called it "give up-itis." The doctors labeled it "marasmus," meaning, "a lack of resistance."

1. Discuss the North Korean POW story and the hate tactics utilized. Why did stirring this type of hatred result in so many deaths?
2. Reflect on the power we possess with our spoken words. How can we be more careful with the things we say?
3. Why do the words "I love you" mean so much to you? If someone says, "I hate you" what impact does it have?

COACHING CONNECTION

For years, I have ended my chapel messages with teams participating in 'shout-outs and gratitudes.' My son Derek calls it 'sharing the love.'

Here's how it works. A shout-out is defined as recognizing someone for what they have done at practice or in a game and a gratitude is pointing out something a person has done away from sports. Players voluntarily identify the person they want to love on. With both people now standing, the rest of the team eavesdrops on the spoken words shared. The exchange is powerful and life-giving as both the one speaking and the one receiving are blessed. Once they are finished, another pair stands up, and then others do as well. This typically goes on for at least a few minutes before closing the chapel time with prayer. Try it out coach—you'll be amazed how energizing it is to see coaches and players loving on one another.

HOSPITALITY

BEARING ONE ANOTHER'S BURDENS

"Dear brothers and sisters, if another believer is overcome by some sin, you who are godly should gently and humbly help that person back onto the right path. And be careful not to fall into the same temptation yourself. Share each other's burdens, and in this way obey the law of Christ." Galatians 6:1-2

Abundant Life Church (Lee's Summit, MO) stated motto is to 'be living proof of a loving God to a watching world.' Their ministry includes an amazing food pantry that serves thousands of people throughout the greater Kansas City metro area every week. The hospitality extended by the volunteers who greet recipients when they arrive by car represents the hands and feet of Jesus. Many who are unchurched are deeply impacted by their active love.

KingdomVideo

American rower Tori Murden has been active in sports all her life. She is an accomplished climber, having summited Alaska's Mount Silverthrone, Mount Kenya in Africa and Antarctica's Lewis Nunatuk—the first-ever summit by a woman. Tori has also completed numerous ice climbing and kayaking expeditions. But she gave up her chance to compete in the Olympics when she gave her equipment to one of her primary competitors as noted on page 42. "The instant I handed [Knox] my riggers," Tori thought, "This is how it is supposed to be. This is why I am here. This is why I trained all that time so that I could actually be here to do something good for somebody else."

Hospitality: Cheerfully sharing food, shelter and my life with others.

1. Identify someone you believe possesses the gift of hospitality. Why did you select this person?
2. Compile a comprehensive list of ways you and your team could demonstrate hospitality in action at your school and in your community.

Team Builder: Select one activity from above which you could do together as a team and get a date on the calendar.

In 1991, Tori dedicated herself to intensive training, vying for a spot in single sculls on the 1992 Olympic Rowing Team. On her drive to Camden, NJ for the trials, Tori was injured in a car accident. Despite being shaken and scrambling to replace her damaged boat, Tori competed. She realized with each race, the effects of the car accident were taking a toll on her performance. At race time, Tori learned fellow rower Michelle Knox had broken the riggers on her scull (riggers hold the scull oars in place) and would be forced to drop out.

Tori chose to forfeit her own chance to compete in the Olympics and donate her equipment to Knox. "[Knox] is one of the finest single scullers in the country," Tori said at the time. Knox placed second in the final race that day and went on to compete in the 1992 Summer Games in Barcelona. Later, after she had offered her rowing equipment to her fellow competitor, Tori discovered she had two broken ribs and a chipped left tibia.

Tori dedicates her life experience, skills and talents to working in areas that are challenging and close to her heart and personal philosophy. The rewards have proven equal to the tasks. While earning her master's degree in divinity from Harvard University, Tori served as a counselor and chaplain at Boston City Hospital and also worked on staff at a homeless services center. Tori considered the field work as a difficult, yet rewarding experience. Later she served in her hometown of Louisville, planning and implementing multi-million-dollar programs designed to revitalize poor and distressed neighborhoods.

The Apostle Paul stated in Galatians 6:2 that we are to 'bear the burdens of one another' as part of our requirements as a believer in Christ. A serving Christian lends a helpful hand with heavy, even crushing, loads which is more than anyone could carry without assistance. This principle not only applies to physical needs, but it includes the heavy, oppressive weight of temptation and spiritual failure. We are not to live under a mindset of self-reliance, but by the commandment to really show we love one another (John 13:34-35).

The early church in Acts also modeled hospitality. In Acts 2 the church actively engaged in caring and sharing of their resources. The love they shared together was completely voluntary. The goods were not evenly distributed but were given to meet needs as they arose. In their fellowship, they broke bread together in their homes and ate together with joy. As a result, the church grew rapidly. Clearly, the Lord is pleased when we show this type of active love.

WEIGHT TRAINING

1. Read Acts 2:42-47. Describe in your own words what was happening in this church. Does the church you attend demonstrate this same type of active love? Why or why not?

2. What does it mean to 'bear the burdens of one another?' Share examples.

3. Why is showing hospitality a big part of a Christian's life? How does hospitality impact those who may not have a relationship with Christ?

4. In defining the fruit (Galatians 5:22-23), Donald Grey Barnhouse in part says, "Love is the key." How is love and hospitality interconnected?

WRAP UP

In his best-seller, *American Caesar*, William Manchester introduces his readers to an in-depth look at World War II hero General Douglas MacArthur. He makes us feel closer to his strong personality as he digs beneath the intimidating exterior and unveils many of MacArthur's magnetic characteristics as well as strange quirks. At one point, the author analyzes the remarkable loyalty that MacArthur elicited from his troops. How did he pull it off? Here is Manchester's analysis in a nutshell:

- He was closer to their age than the other senior officers.
- He shared their discomforts and their danger.
- He adored them in return.

Regardless of the man's well-publicized idiosyncrasies, MacArthur possessed a major redeeming virtue that eclipsed his flaws in his men's eyes and fired their passion: He genuinely and deeply cared for them. The word is LOVE as demonstrated through his hospitality. Nothing ...absolutely nothing, touches people like love. It breaks down internal competition. It makes others feel important. It silences gossip. It builds morale. It promotes feelings that say, "I belong" and "Who cares who gets the credit?" and "I must do my very best" and "You can trust me because I trust you."

Matthew 5:13-16 states, "You are the salt of the earth. But what good is salt if it has lost its flavor? Can you make it salty again? It will be thrown out and trampled underfoot as worthless. You are the light of the world—like a city on a hilltop that cannot be hidden. No one lights a lamp and then puts it under a basket. Instead, a lamp is placed on a stand, where it gives light to everyone in the house. In the same way, let your good deeds shine out for all to see, so that everyone will praise your heavenly Father."

Today, God will place within your sphere of influence a variety of people ranging from dear friends to complete strangers. As He brings people across your path, you will have an opportunity to demonstrate hospitality to each of them. Ultimately, you will have a chance to love them to their full potential as you cultivate a loving relationship. I encourage you to give your heart in unrestrained affection and then watch God work.

1. Read the following verses: Mark 12:31; Romans 12:13; Hebrews 13:2; 1 Peter 4:9; Titus 1:8; 1 Timothy 3:2. What can you learn from these verses about the importance of hospitality?
2. Would you describe yourself as friendly? How do you think others would describe your friendliness?
3. How do you treat total strangers when you first meet them? What are ways you can make total strangers feel more comfortable initially?
4. Think about people you know already. What are a few ways you can make them feel more comfortable or take your relationship to a deeper level? What role does hospitality play in this process?
5. How willing are you to share your possessions with other people? Why do you feel this way? Share an example of when you have been hospitable and a time when you were not. How did you feel after each situation?
6. When you show hospitality, what should you expect in return?

COACHING CONNECTION

Every person has an incredible opportunity to be the hands and feet of Jesus to brothers and sisters who need assistance and help. I often call it being Jesus in skin. It has been said, "People don't care how much you know, until they know how much you care."

The caring I'm talking about is literally helping them 'carry' the issues and burdens that are weighing them down. It is during those times, when people are at their lowest point, when our life and testimony can shine the brightest.

www.kingdomsports.online

PAIN

HESED IS THE PAINKILLER

"For everyone has sinned; we all fall short of God's glorious standard."
Romans 3:23

When Dave Bliss was an NCAA Division I basketball coach, he admittedly allowed the sin of pride to slowly creep into his life. Although he originally got into coaching as a way to help young people mature and grow, he eventually developed an unquenchable thirst for winning and wealth. It all came to a head in 2003 when he was forced to resign as Baylor's head coach amid an ugly scandal which involved illegal payments for players and an attempted cover-up.

KingdomVideo

While suffering through the scandal, Bliss came to an awful realization about the man he had become. He reflects, "I had compromised my integrity and my character and made choices that not only hurt my family, it hurt the school I cared a great deal about. I had a bad metaphor for who God was in my life. And so my daily walk was prone to fail at a certain time. And of course, it hurt a lot of people."

Pain: Experiencing distress, anguish and misery for myself and possibly others through something which has happened.

1. Do you think most injuries are the fault of the individual, the fault of someone else, or accidents that happen for no apparent reason?
2. What are some difficult consequences of getting injured (e.g., physical pain, loss of playing time, disappointment, etc.)?

Team Builder: In every sport, there's always the chance an athlete might get hurt. Have each person share the worst injury they have ever experienced during training, practice or competition.

WARM-UP

In 2017, Bliss retired from coaching at Southwestern Christian U. in Bethany, OK. During his post-Baylor years, he openly shared his story as a warning to others about the pitfalls of his sin. He was thankful for the opportunity to share the hope and restoration found in his renewed relationship with Jesus.

Our world is full of pain. Pain affects us in every way imaginable—physically, emotionally and mentally. While there are many causes, there is really just one true source of pain—sin. Sin is anything separating us from God. It's based in mankind's disobedience and willful turning away from God's plan. No matter how big or small, sin always results in actions that hurt us or others.

In spite of our sin, God wanted to restore His relationship with mankind. Isaiah 54:10 says, "'For the mountains may move and the hills disappear, but even then my faithful love for you will remain. My covenant of blessing will never be broken,' says the Lord, who has mercy on you." The Hebrew word translated as faithful love here is 'hesed.' Theologian John Oswalt says hesed is "complete undeserved kindness and generosity." Hesed is not just a feeling; it's an action. It is an intervention on behalf of those you love by coming to their rescue. God's radical hesed plan was set into motion when He sent His son Jesus to earth. For 33 years, Jesus lived a perfect life as an example to the world. He healed the sick, taught truth to the masses, and set people free from sin. Yet His work wasn't complete until He gave the ultimate sacrifice—His very life.

The crucifixion of Christ is the Bible's most heart-wrenching love story. Even though He was sinless and innocent of any crime, Jesus was sentenced to die in the middle of political and cultural unrest in Israel. He was whipped, beaten, mocked, cursed, and spit on. The Son of God was completely humiliated and mercilessly nailed to a cross, hung high for everyone to see. Why did Jesus subject Himself to this horrific pain? It boils down to one word—hesed!!

Before He died, however, Jesus had a profound conversation with two criminals who were hanging alongside Him (Luke 23:39-43). The first man lashed out in anger, but the other man recognized Jesus as the Messiah and repented of his sin. These men represent two ways we can respond to the sin and pain in our lives. We can either turn further away from God and fall deeper into sin, or we can recognize our brokenness and surrender our hurts to the Savior.

WEIGHT TRAINING

1. Describe a time or a season when you or your team experienced a painful moment. How did this pain impact you and the team?

2. What emotions do you feel as you imagine the events that took place on the day Jesus was crucified? Can you relate to one or both of the criminals in this story? To assist with your answer, watch the 3:52 minute YouTube clip with Pastor Alistair Begg entitled, *The Man On the Middle Cross*.

3. Share your thoughts on this well-known quote from Mother Teresa. "It's okay to have pain in your life, but it's not okay to be one."

WRAP UP

We were born into this world with sin, and Jesus paid the ultimate price so we could be forgiven and restored back to a relationship with the Father. Because of our sin, pain has been a thread running throughout the course of humanity. Thankfully, God has provided three incredible responses to the hopelessness and despair that sin and pain bring into our lives:

1. Jesus suffered pain and even death for your sins. This is the greatest miracle in the history of the world. Jesus willingly chose to step out of His perfect home in heaven and come to earth as a man so He could take on the sins of the world and give us the chance to be with Him in eternity someday. This is love in action. "But God showed his great love for us by sending Christ to die for us while we were still sinners" (Romans 5:8).

2. Jesus can take away your pain. Suffering is inevitable, but it isn't permanent. Jesus can heal our physical, emotional, and mental hurts, and in heaven, the pain we so often experience in this world will be gone forever. "He heals the brokenhearted and bandages their wounds" (Psalm 147:3).

3. Your pain has a purpose. It doesn't always make sense to us why we have to go through so much heartache in our lives, but God brings purpose to our pain and gives us a testimony we can share with others as a result. "And we know that God causes everything to work together for the good of those who love God and are called according to His purpose for them" (Romans 8:28).

There's no escaping pain. Because sin is the one source of all pain and because we were all born with sin, pain and suffering will always be an unfortunate and uncomfortable aspect of our lives. But as we just learned, there is some great news thanks to the sacrifice Jesus made on the cross. While there is no escaping pain there is also no escaping God's faithful love.

In summary, we can look to Jesus. Why?

- **Jesus bore your pain**. His great love for you led Him all the way to the cross.
- **Jesus is the painkiller.** He doesn't want you to be bound by sin or by the consequences of sin. Jesus wants to heal you and set you free.
- **Jesus can use your pain.** He can take those things which have hurt you deeply and change someone else's life for eternity.

1. Identify the three most painful things (physical, emotional, or mental) you have experienced thus far in your life. If you feel comfortable in doing so, share with your teammates. Finding someone you trust with your pain will help in bringing hope and healing.
2. Which of these pains do you need to turn over to God by repenting and asking for forgiveness?
3. Which of the pains do you need to turn over to God by forgiving someone else?
4. Do you believe God can use painful situations in your life to help others and glorify Him? Explain.
5. Comment on this statement. "God has a purpose for your pain, a reason for your struggle and a reward for your faithfulness. Don't give up!"

COACHING CONNECTION

Today, you can rely on God's 'hesed' for you no matter what you face. Why is this true? Jesus Christ took the penalty of sin upon Himself when He went to the cross for all mankind. Through His sacrifice, He won the ultimate victory over sin. He defeated sin and offered forgiveness, restoration, and healing to anyone and everyone. A life-changing relationship with God begins with having a personal relationship with the Son of God. He desires to take your hurts and heal you with His perfect love. Through Him, complete healing and restoration are available to anyone who calls upon His name.

www.kingdomsports.online

PASSION

LAYING IT ALL OUT FOR HIM

"Those who belong to Christ Jesus have nailed the passions and desires of their sinful nature to His cross and crucified them there." Galatians 5:24

On June 19, 1986, Maryland basketball star Len Bias died of cocaine intoxication two days after being selected by the Boston Celtics as the second overall pick in the NBA draft. His mother, Lonise Bias, had no idea he was using the drug. Since his death, Lonise has been on a passionate crusade, conducting workshops and seminars around the USA in an effort to stop drug abuse among our nation's youth.

KingdomVideo

Lonise is an internationally-known motivational speaker, trainer, consultant and family life coach. Bias launched her campaign 35 years ago to cope with her loss and to help parents avoid similar tragedy. "I have seen a lot of good come out of his death. I believe Len's death helped turn the situation around involving drugs. Len lost his life to help save others."

Passion: Having an intense, powerful or compelling emotion and feelings toward others or something.

1. Lonise Bias has been passionate about sharing her son's tragic story with anyone and everyone. Why do you think she is so passionate about sharing the story?
2. Lonise also said, "If Len would have lived he would have entertained you. But in death, he brought life." How can this be true?

Team Builder: As a team, search on YouTube and watch a portion of a famous sermon 'That's My King' delivered by Dr. S.M. Lockridge. Scenes from *The Passion of the Christ* are shown in the background of an extended version (7:07) and short version (3:19). Lockridge was the pastor of a prominent African-American congregation in San Diego, CA from 1953 to 1993. He was known for his passionate preaching style all around the world. After viewing, discuss the passion of Dr. Shadrach Meshach Lockridge.

I love to be around people who are passionate about life and athletics. People with passion have energy and an attitude that brings out the best in others. Andy Andrews said, "Passion is a product of the heart. Passion is what helps you when you have a dream. Passion breeds conviction and turns mediocrity into excellence! Your passion will motivate others to join you in pursuit of your dream. With passion, you will overcome insurmountable obstacles. You will become unstoppable!"

Throughout my lifetime, I have had the privilege of being around people of passion, and I have always benefited greatly from them. While I have never met Lonise Bias, I know I would like her because she is passionate about helping people.

To see passion personified, we need only to look at Jesus Christ. The word 'passion' comes from a Latin word meaning 'suffering.' The suffering He endured could not have been any more horrific. Even before the Roman guards captured Him in the Garden of Gethsemane, He was sweating drops of blood (Luke 22:44). He literally took the sins of the entire world, past, present and future, upon Himself by experiencing the worst death possible—crucifixion.

Only the worst criminals were crucified. Yet it was even more dreadful for Jesus because He was nailed to the cross by His hands and feet rather than tied to the cross to speed up His death. Each nail was 6 to 8 inches long and was driven into His wrists and His bound feet. There's a tendon in the wrist that extends to the shoulder. The Roman guards knew when the nails were being hammered into the wrist, the tendon would tear and break, forcing Jesus to use His back muscles to support Himself, so He could breathe. For hours on the cross, Jesus endured incredible pain and suffering with each breath.

The beatings, the taunts from the crowd, the gruesome walk on the Viva Delarosa to Calvary, and the nails driven into His hands and feet were all part of God's supreme plan to save mankind. His passion for you and me was what gave Him the will to go to the cross for our sins. Love for mankind is what drove His passion.

One of the most stunning statements Jesus ever made was about His own death and resurrection is in John 10:17-18. Jesus chose to die. He embraced it because of His complete obedience to His Father. Read Philippians 2:5-11.

WEIGHT TRAINING

1. Besides Jesus, who is the most passionate person you know? What do you think fuels their passion?

2. What are you passionate about?

3. Read John 10:7-18. How does the passion of Jesus impact you?

4. Why did Jesus have to die on the cross?

WRAP UP

John Piper said, "Because of this unparalleled passion, God raised Jesus from the dead. It happened three days later. Early Sunday morning, He rose from the dead. He appeared numerous times to His disciples for forty days before His ascension to heaven (Acts 1:3). Jesus finished the work God gave Him to do, and the resurrection was the proof that God was satisfied. His resurrection proved we were now free from the bondage of death. We are now fully reconciled to God."

The passion of Jesus Christ is the most important event in history, and to this day it is still the most explosive topic on planet earth. His death and resurrection is the centerpiece of God's entire plan. The apostle Paul recognized the importance of these events when he penned his words as noted 1 Corinthians 15:13-17, "For if there is no resurrection of the dead, then Christ has not been raised either. And if Christ has not been raised, then all our preaching is useless, and your faith is useless. And we apostles would all be lying about God—for we have said that God raised Christ from the grave. But that can't be true if there is no resurrection of the dead. And if there is no resurrection of the dead, then Christ has not been raised. And if Christ has not been raised, then your faith is useless and you are still guilty of your sins." To put it bluntly, Paul stated this truth: "We are all idiots for believing in Jesus if the resurrection didn't happen."

The apostles, who saw Jesus after His death and resurrection, clearly knew based on firsthand evidence that He was alive. Paul tells us there were over

500 witnesses of the Resurrected Christ. Every disciple, except for John who the authorities tried to kill in a boiling vat of oil and eventually was exiled to the island of Patmos, willingly died for Him as a martyr. According to tradition, Peter was crucified upside down because he felt unworthy to die in the same manner as Jesus. In fact, His passion became their passion. Without this assurance, they would have scattered in many directions trying to save their own skin. Instead, they were martyred themselves, thus perpetuating the truth about Jesus Christ.

Years ago during my senior year of high school, I was impacted greatly by a sophomore on my football team. He understood and lived out the passion of Jesus Christ. When he practiced or played, he imagined Jesus Christ sitting in the bleachers watching his every move. His passion to perform for Jesus Christ was his only motivation. He gave effort that exceeded the entire team. I saw this young athlete work, sweat and compete for the glory of God. This sophomore's passion changed me and our entire team.

1. Read the crucifixion story found in the Gospels (Matthew 27-28 is one of the accounts). Discuss this event and why it was deemed important by the authorities to claim the body was stolen. Why the cover-up? Why is this story the most important historical event of all time?
2. How about you? Are you willing to lay everything out on the field because Jesus Christ laid it all out for you? If so, your passion will impact people for eternity.
3. *The Passion of the Christ* is a powerful movie of Jesus' final hours before He died on the cross. Watch this movie as a team and discuss the passion of Jesus Christ.

COACHING CONNECTION

Passion can be very positive if directed correctly. The most influential players on your team are probably the ones who have the most passion because they will do anything and everything to help their team excel. Who is the most passionate athlete you have ever coached? What was the driving force of his/her passion?

We are warned in 2 Timothy 2:22 to flee from youthful passions, and instead pursue righteousness, faith, love and peace from a pure heart. When passion is Christ-centered, you will experience Him fully and completely. A relentless passionate pursuit of Christ will result in the abundant life He promises (John 10:10).

PURITY

STAYING CLEAR FROM FILTH

"Even children are known by the way they act, whether their conduct is pure, and whether it is right." Proverbs 20:11

Sexual misconduct issues are currently in the sports headlines regarding decades of abuse that took place with the University of Michigan athletic program. In a January 2021 court filing, more than 850 former students reported being molested during routine physicals or other visits. This comes on the heels of a $500 million settlement with Michigan State University over abuse by sports doctor Larry Nassar. In addition, Ohio State University has paid more than $45 million to 185 people who said they were groped by another sports doctor.

KingdomVideo

Without exception, I have found over the years the entry point for inappropriate sexual activity, including pre-marital sex, masturbation, adultery, and so much more, begins with looking at pornographic images. Pornography results in impurity. This Workout will address an area that is destroying individuals and marriages. I encourage you to live a pure life in an impure world.

Purity: Freeing yourself from anything that contaminates or adulterates.

1. Why are conversations about purity issues so uncomfortable, awkward, embarrassing and even taboo?
2. How well does your church or Christian ministry talk about purity issues? What are they doing right and wrong?

Team Builder: Prior to the meeting, have several students interview at least one married person (perhaps a youth pastor) who waited until after the marriage ceremony to have sex. Ask the married person for the keys to staying pure and the benefits they are reaping today from their commitment to purity. Share the positive and negative results with the entire group.

Ezra really impresses me. Here was a man who was responsible for rebuilding the city of Jerusalem after King Nebuchadnezzar and the Babylonian empire destroyed it. Israel simply "reaped what they sowed" as they were warned numerous times about the devastating consequences of their sins. Among the many sins they committed, they were impure. They intermarried with foreigners. Godly traditions were exchanged for filth. Their form of worship became bowing down to idols and false gods. Ezra stepped into this mess and dealt with these issues of impurity. He initiated a cleansing process, and the restoration of Jerusalem began to take place under his leadership. Read Ezra 9:1-15 and 10:1-17 for details.

One area where it is particularly easy to become impure is succumbing to sexual temptation. God's Word deals directly with this issue and the perils involved when we do not rely on Christ's power and His promises. Romans 13:14 tells us "to not gratify the desires of the sinful nature." 1 Corinthians 6:18 reminds us to "flee from sexual immorality." We are pounded with impurity messages via the Internet, television, movies, smartphones, magazines, and at the beach, park or mall. Certainly there are things we can do to protect us from impurity.

Sex is not love and love is not sex. Remember, God is not anti-sex. The truth is He designed and created sex, and it is a beautiful thing reserved exclusively for a man and a woman who are married. Hebrews 13:4 clearly states God's judgment on immorality and the adulterous.

Jerry Kirk says, "Choosing to let Jesus be in control of your sex life will shape every other area of your life because sexuality is at the center of our being. This decision will influence your current and future ability as a husband (or wife), father (or mother) and Christian. Choosing purity is difficult, but for those who put in the hard work and prayer, living by Christ's standard is a road to deep joy and real sexual satisfaction."

Randy Alcorn says this about purity. "Purity is always smart; impurity is always stupid. Not sometimes. Not usually. Always. You're not an exception. I'm not an exception. There are no exceptions." Randy points out in his book, *The Purity Principle*, that embracing purity is to claim a magnificent gift. He says, "To choose purity is to put yourself under God's blessing. To choose impurity is to put yourself under God's curse." Those are pretty big stakes!!

WEIGHT TRAINING

1. How would you define 'purity' and 'impurity?' Why does God highly regard purity and condemn impurity?

2. Identify places or things you believe are impure. Compare your list of items to what others have identified. Are you surprised what is and isn't on your list?

3. What are some of the keys to remaining pure?

WRAP UP

"If it feels good..." you can finish the sentence. The temptation of sexual pleasure outside of marriage represents the desire to be sensually satisfied no matter the cost. It may appear harmless initially, but sexual contact with anyone other than your spouse is an illicit sexual encounter. The inappropriate act is not the only issue; the attitude is the primary problem. "I want what I want when I want it. I am going to be happy. I need to be fulfilled; my sexual desires will be gratified...regardless!"

We may never come out and say it this boldly, but we probably are thinking this way. In doing so we rationalize Scriptural truth, we lower our standard of morality, and we ignore the promptings of our conscience. We convince ourselves it is not merely okay; it is a necessity! And if somehow conviction from a holy God interrupts the fun, we have ways of ignoring Him, too. Paul portrays such people as 'fools' (Romans 1:21-22).

Daily we are told sex outside of marriage is normal and a sign of true love. Our own longings for love and our God-given passions push us toward physical expressions of our feelings. But controlling passion is the best way to keep it strong and growing, even when you want to marry the person. According to the Bible, the boundaries of sex are the boundaries of marriage. Sex and marriage go together. Honor God by staying pure—honor Him with your body (1 Corinthians 6:19-20).

Finally, the battle for purity is won or lost in direct correlation between the time you spend with God versus the time you spend looking at pornography or thinking about lustful issues. The more time you are seeking the Lord, the less time you'll put yourself in the wrong places. Randy Alcorn said, "Do you want freedom from the actions and obsessions of lust? Get help. Be wise. Avoid temptation. Go to Christ. Experience His sufficiency. Draw on His power. Depend on Him one day at a time. Never underestimate Christ. Sin is not more powerful than God." This is good news for the person who wants to experience victory (1 John 5:4).

1. Read Proverbs 22:11; Philippians 4:8; Titus 1:15; James 1:14-15; 1 Corinthians 10:12-13; and 1 Thessalonians 4:3-7. Based on these verses, what are some of the principles God gives us regarding temptations and proper sexual conduct? What are the results of a pure heart?

2. How have you chosen purity over immoral behavior at school? In sports? On TV? On your cell phone? At your job?

3. God created sex to be reserved solely for our mate within the context of marriage. How does sexual purity honor God? How does sexual purity bless us?

4. What are the keys to remaining sexually pure? (Note for parents: This would be an excellent place to discuss abstinence with your children. Why? Experts tell us the average age of children exposed to pornographic images and inappropriate sexual misconduct is now eight years old).

COACHING CONNECTION

Coach—are you living a pure life in an impure world? What are the keys to being pure? As a person of great stature in your school and community, you have a tremendous responsibility and calling to live a life of purity.

According to *Every Man's Battle*, "You are sexually pure when no sexual gratification comes from anyone or anything but your spouse." In this sex-crazed culture, one of the ways you can truly honor the Lord is by only pursuing your spouse. You and your spouse, your children and grandchildren, along with the team you lead will be truly blessed when you make this commitment. Pursue purity—it is always the best!

RESURRECTION

LIAR, LUNATIC OR LORD?

"And if Christ has not been raised, then your faith is useless and you are still guilty of your sins." 1 Corinthians 15:17

Tommy John surgery, more formally known as ulnar collateral ligament (UCL) reconstruction, is used to repair a torn ligament inside the elbow. A number of athletes, and specifically baseball pitchers, have successfully resurrected their careers after UCL repair. The surgery was first performed in 1974 on Los Angeles Dodgers pitcher Tommy John, who was in the middle of his best pro season before suffering permanent damage to his UCL. This would usually have been a career-ending injury, but thanks to the procedure named after him, thousands of baseball pitchers have had their careers resurrected and many of them pitch with even greater velocity. The recovery time from Tommy John surgery can take up to 18 months. While it's amazing to watch a pitcher's career resurrected through an innovative surgery, think how incredible it was for Jesus' disciples to witness His resurrection.

Resurrection: Miraculously witnessing someone or something coming back to life after it is pronounced dead.

1. A resurrection doesn't happen through luck, coincidence or good fortune. Have you seen something come back to life after it was dead? If so, describe what happened and the impact it had on you or others.
2. Read 1 Corinthians 15:1-34. Paul states all of Christianity hinges on the resurrection of Jesus Christ. Why did Paul believe this to be true?

Team Builder: A number of skeptics, including Lee Strobel and Josh McDowell, have unsuccessfully tried to refute Christianity by researching the facts centered on the resurrection of Jesus Christ. Have one or more of your team members, or a local pastor, present their findings and have a healthy debate on this subject.

The historical record of Jesus' death, burial and resurrection is found in the writings of the Gospel writers—Matthew, Mark, Luke and John. He was mercilessly mocked, beaten and whipped, and then finally put to death (John 19). From the time of Jesus' arrest in the Garden of Gethsemane through the early hours on Sunday morning, the disciples' emotions were filled with confusion, fear and hopelessness. Their leader, the supposed Messiah, was dead. Their dreams were shattered. What would they do now?

Even though Jesus told them He would rise from the dead, they had a difficult time believing it was true when they received the news of His resurrection. Thomas, one of the disciples, said he wouldn't believe it unless he was able to put his fingers on Jesus' wounds which he ultimately did and It fully convinced him of Jesus' resurrection (John 20:24-29). For 40 days prior to Jesus' ascension, He revealed His resurrected body to over 500 witnesses, including the disciples. During this time, He authenticated His life's purpose and message. Christianity is based on the person of Jesus Christ, and the most important event in history is the resurrection. If Christ's existence and His resurrection didn't happen, then there is no Christianity.

The missing body of Jesus resulted in a major cover-up story by the Roman and Jewish authorities, as documented in Matthew 28. The claim of the disciples stealing the body sometime prior to early Sunday morning is ridiculous. Do you really think it's possible for these scared disciples to overpower a highly skilled and trained 24-man Roman squadron? These soldiers knew they would be killed immediately if anything happened to the dead body of Jesus. A Roman seal guaranteed nothing would happen. Further, if the disciples had a dead body, do you think it would've been possible for all of them to keep a secret hidden all the way to their own deaths? Think about it—someone would have broken Why? Because it is human nature to save your own neck.

Chuck Colson, "I know the resurrection is a fact, and Watergate proved it to me. How? Because 12 men testified they had seen Jesus raised from the dead, then they proclaimed that truth for 40 years, never once denying it. Everyone was beaten, tortured, stoned and put into prison. They would not have endured that if it weren't true. Watergate embroiled 12 of the most powerful men in the world—and they couldn't keep a lie for three weeks. You're telling me 12 apostles could keep a lie for 40 years? Absolutely impossible."

WEIGHT TRAINING

1. Read Matthew 28 and talk about the various theories surrounding the missing body of Jesus. Why are all these theories not true?

2. How does the Watergate story from 50+ years ago authenticate the resurrection story?

3. In what ways does the resurrection of Jesus impact your athletic career?

4. How does Jesus' resurrection challenge you to live differently than the world?

WRAP UP

The courage of the post-resurrection disciples is one of the clearest evidences this entire story is true. Every single disciple, except for the Apostle John, died a martyr's death—beheaded, stoned, beaten, crucified and pierced with spears. In 95 A.D., John was the last remaining apostle alive. The Roman Emperor announced, "Lions don't always kill them and there have been times the fire doesn't burn their bodies. Cutting off their heads is too noble of an end. So let's throw John in a vat of boiling oil...no one could survive that!" Yet, John did in a glorious fashion. He ended up being exiled to the island of Patmos where he wrote the book of Revelation. He died at peace in 101 A.D. in Ephesus.

During my freshman year in college, I had the opportunity to hear Josh McDowell deliver a compelling talk on the resurrection of Jesus. Over the past 50 years, McDowell has given 27,200 talks to over 25,200,000 people in 126 countries, primarily speaking on the resurrection. His groundbreaking book, *Evidence That Demands a Verdict* is recognized as one of the 20th century's top 40 books! Little has changed in his approach during the past five decades when he speaks on the resurrection. Here are a few of his notable quotes:

- "After more than 700 hours of studying this subject, and thoroughly investigating its foundation, I have come to the conclusion the resurrection of Jesus Christ is one of the most wicked, vicious, heartless hoaxes ever foisted upon the minds of men, or it is the most fantastic fact of history."

- "Few people seem to realize the resurrection of Jesus is the cornerstone to a worldview that provides the perspective of all of life."
- "No matter how devastating our struggles, disappointments, and troubles, they are only temporary. No matter what happens to you, no matter the depth of tragedy or pain you face, no matter how death stalks you, the resurrection promises you a future of immeasurable good."

Without the resurrection, Jesus' death would go without divine interpretation and endorsement. The resurrection amounts to the Father's clear signal that Jesus is the powerful Son of God who has conquered death and reigns as Lord of all (Romans 1:4; 4:25). It means union with Jesus Christ now and in the future. God no longer sees our unrighteousness but sees us through the righteousness of Christ. We are freed from the presence and power of sin. Jesus' power brings light into darkness. The resurrection proves Jesus is the Christ (Messiah) and the Son of God. It authenticates everything He said and did.

1. Why do you think Jesus was so driven to do whatever it took to follow through with God's plan? Consider the impact of love in your answer.
2. Respond to this statement. "Jesus can only be one of three things—Liar, Lunatic or Lord. Every person needs to put Jesus in one of these three categories. There are no other options."
3. What are some dreams you have already surrendered to God? What are dreams you still need to surrender to God? What is holding you back?

COACHING CONNECTION

Jesus defeated death and rose again so He could offer us the gift of eternal life (John 11:25 and 1Corinthians 15:3-6). Today, Jesus is alive. Do you believe this is true?

The resurrection of Jesus Christ gives us the ultimate victory over death and the grave. Without Christ's resurrection and death would be the ultimate defeat. No event in history comes close to the resurrection story. The power of death has been overcome by Christ! Knowing Jesus died, was buried, and rose from the dead victorious over sin, death, and the grave should motivate us to coach and live our lives dedicated to the work of the Lord.

www.kingdomsports.online

TRUST

TRUST BEGINS WITH CHRIST

"I trust in God, so why should I be afraid? What can mere mortals do to me?"
Psalm 56:11

In most sports, athletes are required to change directions quickly, and going the wrong direction can be costly. Take, for instance, former NFL star Jim Marshall, who spent 20 years in the league. Even though Marshall was a two-time Pro Bowl selection, he is most noted for the mistake he made in 1964 when his Minnesota Vikings were playing the San Francisco 49ers. After recovering a fumble, Marshall ran 66 yards to the wrong end zone. Thinking he had scored a touchdown, he tossed the ball out of bounds and gave the opposing team a safety and two points.

KingdomVideo

Thankfully for Marshall, Minnesota still won the game, but his legacy is now wrapped up in his one infamous mistake instead of a long and successful career. After this mistake, Marshall was known around the NFL as 'Wrong Way Marshall.' However, when he retired after playing a record-setting 302 straight games, his teammates called him 'Old Indestructible' because they could depend upon him.

Trust: Believing completely and totally in someone or something.

1. Which sports require the greatest amount of trust among teammates in order to be successful? Share examples supporting your view.
2. Who is someone you trust on your team? Why?
3. Do you consider yourself trustworthy? Why or why not?

Team Builder: Pair everyone up and have one person on each team blindfolded, with their partner directing them through an obstacle course while holding the other person's hand or arm. Have the entire team discuss what they learned regarding trust.

WARM-UP

All game changers have an uncanny ability to make big plays—clutch shots, diving catches, or spectacular saves, causing a major momentum shift in the direction of a contest. From God's perspective, the ultimate game-changing play takes place when we make a radical change of direction by turning away from a life of sin and turning toward a relationship with His Son, Jesus Christ.

Former MLB outfielder Josh Hamilton knows something about going the wrong direction, except his blunder didn't happen on the baseball diamond. As a promising Major League prospect, an injury took Hamilton out of commission and led him down a destructive path of alcohol and drug abuse. He shares words of warning, "As an athlete, it is such a rush on the field making a good play, doing things that most people can't do. And it felt like the drugs did that for me. When I didn't have baseball, it made me get that rush and made me feel like I was on top of the world. But it always ended badly."

Josh's wake-up call came when the league suspended him multiple times for failing drug tests and later when some people close to him, including a mentor and his grandmother, helped the troubled athlete by giving him some tough love. "I think the main thing [my story] demonstrates is once you allow God to come into your life, He always has a plan for your life," Hamilton says. "He stands faithful if you trust Him. He is always there for you, no matter what you go through, no matter if you stray away from Him. He is going to be there, and He will always be there just waiting for you to come back and waiting to do great things with your life when you make the decision to live for Him." The game changer in Hamilton's life was his repentant attitude, which led to saving faith in Jesus Christ.

Many times, a coach gets our attention through tough love by calling us out. The coach might scold us for not giving our best effort in practice, making us run laps. The coach might bark instructions from the sideline loudly enough for everyone in the stands to hear. The coach might even sit us on the bench or, worse, kick us off the team for an attitude issue or for breaking a team rule.

I have often said, "Tough love is real love, and without tough love, you don't actually love at all." Proverbs 27:6 says, "Wounds from a sincere friend are better than many kisses from an enemy." Beware of those who are kissing up to you, and not speaking the truth in love. Can you really trust them? Remember, trust is the glue for all healthy relationships.

WEIGHT TRAINING

1. What are some decisions people make that lead them in wrong directions? Discuss these decisions and their consequence.

2. Have you ever experienced tough love? How did tough love ultimately help you?

3. Have you placed your trust and faith in Jesus Christ as Lord and Savior? If not, what has prevented you from repenting of your sin and placing your trust and faith in Him?

WRAP UP

Is it easy to trust God? The fact is, nothing is more difficult in certain times and circumstances. What happens to us when a horrific experience rocks our trust? Does our faith in God overcome the intense pain? Are we so dazed we can't even see God? Many things work to blot out our trust, including discouragement, disappointments, persecutions, misunderstandings, failures, or unfulfilled dreams and ambitions. Where is God in times of trouble? Pastor and author Bruce Larson says he grew up saying yes to biblical doctrines, but eventually he sensed God was asking him a deeper question, "Will you trust Me with your life? Yes, or no?"

Jesus trusted God. No matter what He faced He said, "Thy will be done." Defeat itself could not daunt Him or make Him drawback. If we desire to be trustworthy, we must begin by having resolute trust in God and in God alone, just like Jesus Christ. Trust is built through the belief God knows what is best for your life. God simply asks us to trust Him in keeping His promises. He asks us to let go of reasons, rights, and fears and simply throw our arms around Him. As our trust and dependence upon Him deepen, and as we grow in our integrity and love, we will become trustworthy in our daily lives.

One of the most radical accounts of a direction change can be found in Acts 9. There, we read about a man named Saul, a powerful Jewish leader who made it his mission to persecute all Jews who now followed the teachings of Jesus and Ananias, a devoted follower of Christ. Like Saul, who would later be renamed Paul, we too are being called out by God. For some of us, it's the call to salvation—a first encounter with Him where we turn from our sin and place our faith and trust in Him as Savior and Lord. For others, it might be the need to rededicate our lives to Christ. Maybe we've accepted Him in the past but allowed sin or apathy to take us off the right path. For all of us, God is calling us to repentance and placing our trust in Him.

Repentance is turning away from sinful, selfish behavior and walking with Him toward righteousness and selflessness. Perhaps today God is calling you to take this game changing step. Jesus became the ultimate game-changer when He died on the cross in order to pay for our sin (John 3:16). Before we can become a game changer for Him, we must first recognize our need for salvation through the blood of Christ. Have you ever wondered how you could make things right with God? If so, read *More than Winning* on page 95.

1. Read Acts 9:1-22. What extreme measures did God use to call out Saul and encourage Ananias?
2. What are some of the obstacles that stop us from trusting completely in God? Why is it hard to trust God?
3. What is the evidence of a life that trusts God?
4. In what ways have you seen trust work on your team? What happens when there is a lack of trust on your team?
5. Have you ever been let down by someone? Ever thought you were going to make the team but were cut instead? Or have you shared something in complete confidence only to learn your confidence was betrayed? How about a friend who offered to help with a project and then bailed out? Describe how you feel when someone breaks your trust.

COACHING CONNECTION

We build trust with others each time we choose (1) Integrity over image: committing to be the right person and do the right thing. An arrogant ego makes us untrustworthy; (2) Truth over convenience: committing to speak the truth instead of half-truths or white lies; (3) Love over personal gain: committing to serve others rather than serving ourselves.

Former PepsiCo Chairman and CEO Craig Weatherup explains it this way, "You don't build trust by talking about it. You build it by achieving results, always with integrity and in a manner that shows real personal regard for the people with whom you work." As noted here, two pillars make trust possible—integrity and love.

TRUTH

TRUTH ALWAYS BEATS LIES

"It (love) does not rejoice about injustice but rejoices whenever the truth wins out." 1 Corinthians 13:6

Failure happens. Even in an undefeated season, there will be fumbles, interceptions, errors, turnovers and missed shots, but often in the sports world, failure within a game, a season or an entire career unfairly dictates how athletes feel about themselves. We sometimes believe our worth is wrapped up in our performance or successes. This couldn't be further from the truth. There are many more lies we can believe if we're not careful, but whether we're dealing with sports or just everyday life, the truth of Jesus Christ always overcomes lies and serves as a key component in our quest to understand our true identity.

KingdomVideo

At the end of your life, the honors, awards, trophies and championships will not matter one iota and neither will the defeats. Everything will boil down to your personal relationship with Jesus Christ. He loved you before you were even born. As Jeremiah 29:11 states, "For I know the plans I have for you," says the LORD. "They are plans for good and not for disaster, to give you a future and a hope."

Truth: Believing accurate and documented facts.

1. How good are you at telling whether or not someone is being truthful with you?
2. What factors help you decide what is true and what is untrue?

Team Builder: Choose several volunteers to play a game of deception. The selected individual(s) should tell three things about themselves, two of which are true and one is false. The rest of the group determines which of the three statements is the lie. Was it easy or difficult to discern the truth from the lies? Explain.

When snowboarder Kelly Clark took a hard fall at the 2006 Torino Winter Olympics, it took her out of medal contention, yet the defending 2002 half-pipe gold medalist experienced overwhelming peace amid the disappointment. Why? Early in her career, Kelly Clark believed the lie that her identity and self-worth could only be found in the sport of snowboarding and her performance. It was in December 2004 that Clark, then a 20-year-old phenom, discovered the truth. At the time she was contemplating quitting snowboarding altogether, she met another young lady who shared God's love with her.

Through this encounter, Clark learned she had bought into a lie. She was never meant to have her identity wrapped up in snowboarding. Once consumed by her performance within the sport, she began to understand she was created to be a child of God and her true identity was found in a relationship with Christ. Second Corinthians 5:17 says, "This means that anyone who belongs to Christ has become a new person. The old life is gone; a new life has begun!"

Understanding this truth allowed Clark to experience freedom in her sport. She was no longer bound to the lie that her self-worth could only be found in athletic success. No longer held captive to the world's expectations for her life, she could now turn all the pressure to succeed over to God.

At the 2014 Winter Games in Sochi, Clark was once again the favorite to win gold, but when her performance was only good enough for the bronze medal, she counted it a blessing. Her new identity in Christ was on full display for a watching world to see. "There's no place where you can get freedom apart from Him," Clark said. "I've brought that freedom into my snowboarding. It really does set me apart from a lot of the athletes. I get to do what I love with the One that I love." Your true identity is knowing and understanding WHO you are and WHOSE you are. At the foundation of identity, you are a child of God who is loved deeply.

Perhaps you've experienced lies in your athletic career or in your personal life. Maybe you've heard some other lies we will discuss in a moment. But here's the truth; Satan is the father of lies and God is not just the creator of truth—He *is* truth. Lies are based on hate and destruction, while truth is based on love. 1 Corinthians 13:6 points out the difference between the truth and lies, and it all comes back to love.

WEIGHT TRAINING

1. Have you ever been too wrapped up in your sport? If so, explain what it looked like and how it impacted your life.

2. Read John 8:31-38, 42-47. Why is truth and love so important when it comes to being set free?

3. Read Ephesians 6:17 and 1 John 2:14. These verses talk about the power God's Word gives us. What are some ways you can use God's truth to overcome Satan's lies?

WRAP UP

Satan has been lying to mankind since the beginning of time. He was a fallen angel who foolishly tried to overthrow God. After the first man and woman were created, Satan disguised himself as a serpent and convinced them to disobey their Creator (Genesis 3:1-7).

Remember these key truth points:
- **Satan is the father of lies.** Since his fall from Heaven, Satan has perpetuated lies and deception against mankind. He will do and say anything within his power to separate you from your Creator. Read John 8:44 and Revelation 12:9.
- **Some of Satan's lies include:** "God doesn't really love me," "I've done too many bad things to be saved," "I'm worthless," "I'm only as good as my performance," and "I can't do anything right."
- **God is the truth. God embodies truth and cannot lie.** He wants you to believe and embrace the truth so you can have a fulfilling relationship with Him. Read Hebrews 6:17-18 and James 1:17-18. God's truth is spoken in John 3:16; Ephesians 2:8-9; Psalm 139:13-14; Philippians 4:13; Romans 10:13; and numerous other passages.

Since Adam and Eve ushered sin into this world, Satan has been doing his best to keep man separated from God. Satan's first words in the Bible are seen in Genesis 3:1 when he asked Eve, "Did God really say....? This line has been repeated over and over throughout the ages to undermine God's truth statements. Here is a truth statement you can take to the bank which I have been telling people for years and years: "God loves you and He has a wonderful plan for your life; and Satan hates you and has a hell of a plan for your life."

Even Jesus was not immune to this sort of temptation. In fact, the devil attempted three times to trick the Son of God into sinful behavior with his trademark words of deception. In Matthew 4:1-11, Satan tried to entice Jesus into sinning by twisting God's truth. In the second temptation, Satan even quoted Scripture to try and get Jesus to sin. Jesus combated the deception and temptation through speaking powerful Scriptural truths back to him.

1. Read Matthew 4:1-11 and discuss the three ways Satan tried to tempt Jesus. To which parts of Jesus' humanity do you think he was trying to appeal? How did Jesus respond to each of these temptations? Why do you think His response matters to us?

2. According to John 8:44, the devil has been a murderer and a liar from the beginning. What are some of Satan's lies noted above that you have personally fought against? What are some other lies you've heard? Why does Satan want to separate you from God and His truth?

3. Do you ever struggle to embrace God's Word as the truth? If so, why?

4. What do you think a real love relationship with God might look like? What lies are separating you from Him?

5. Here's an undeniable truth—'God loves you and has a wonderful plan for your life; and Satan hates you and has a hell of a plan for your life.' How does this truth make you feel?

COACHING CONNECTION

The coaches I respect greatly are those who are committed to speaking and living out truth. Truth delivered in love is what inspires and encourages a team. Deception and sharing lies destroys team chemistry and any chance of being successful.

When Jesus responded to Satan in Matthew 4, He didn't enter into a debate or take time to contemplate what His enemy had to say. Instead, Jesus quickly quoted from God's Word demonstrating how to use an unbeatable tool in the fight against Satan's lies. In Ephesians 6:17, Paul describes God's Word as "the sword of the Spirit," and in 1 John 2:14, John says if we have God's Word in us, "you have had victory over the evil one." In John 14:6, Jesus boldly proclaims, "I am the way, the truth, and the life. No one can come to the Father except through Me." Not only does God's truth bring freedom, it also guarantees our eternal victory in the battle against Satan's lies.

WORTH

GOD IS ALL IN

"So God created human beings in His own image. In the image of God He created them; male and female He created them." Genesis 1:27

Sold-out athletes never waver in competition, they don't look back, and they are consumed with a single goal. When an athlete is all in—body, mind, and heart—there are no limits on what can be accomplished. A sold-out relationship with Jesus Christ requires you to be all in as well. Every thought, word, and action is to glorify the Savior. No looking back; it's time to take a step of faith and commit 100% to your Coach, Jesus Christ. When you are all in, there is no limit to what God can accomplish through you.

KingdomVideo

All in. That simple two-word phrase is the battle cry of all athletes who are willing to do whatever it takes to achieve greatness. Athletes who go all in are fully committed to a singular goal. They will make personal sacrifices to maximize their potential in order to obtain the prize.

Worth: Having great value and importance.

1. What are the primary factors in determining how much something is worth?
2. What are the different ways people determine the worth of others?

Team Builder: Everyone sit in a circle and take a minute to check out the area in your immediate surroundings. Identify the most valuable item in the area. Once everyone has found something, go around the circle and have each individual determine his or her item's worth. What factors help you decide what something is worth?

Long before humans began competing against each other in this thing we call 'sport,' God went all in for us. He created the universe and this place we call home. He lovingly crafted us in His image and gave us a purpose that runs much deeper than our accomplishments and far outweighs our failures. God's love has nothing to do with our performance and everything to do with our very existence. We have value because we are His creation. From the beginning of time until this very moment, God has always gone all in for you!

Jackie Robinson is one of history's greatest examples of an athlete who was willing to go all in. By 1941, for instance, he had become the first person to earn letters in four sports at UCLA, but Robinson is most noted for his courageous battle against racial inequality within Major League Baseball. In 1945, Brooklyn Dodgers general manager and president Branch Rickey (who later became one of FCA's founding fathers) signed the African-American second baseman to a contract. In 1947, Robinson made history as the first black MLB player in the modern era, debut amid an intense flurry of racial epithets and public opposition. Through it all, Robinson maintained his dignity and bravely hoped for a time when people would see deeper than his skin color. He knew his value wasn't wrapped up in his performance on the baseball diamond but rather based solely on the fact he was a child of God.

Rickey, who likewise had a strong faith in God and relied heavily on his relationship with Jesus in order to fight the racial prejudice of those days, said, "I couldn't face my God much longer knowing that His black creatures are held separate and distinct from His white creatures in the game that has given me all I own." Rickey's determination to do something about prejudice in baseball began when he was managing a team when a black player was not allowed to stay at a hotel with the team. Rickey was able to get him into the hotel for the night, but he never forgot the incident and later said, "I may not be able to do something about racism in every field, but I can sure do something about it in baseball." Rickey took a bold stance against racism and it was a major breakthrough for our nation.

Jackie understood his self-worth despite what society was telling him at the time. As a believer in Jesus Christ, Jackie Robinson knew there was no person, no power and no problem that could stand against God and His plan.

WEIGHT TRAINING

1. What are some characteristics Jackie Robinson likely relied on as he went all in as a pioneering baseball player?

2. Read Genesis 1:27. What does the phrase "created...in his own image" personally mean to you?

3. Read Psalm 139:13-16. How is our worth in God's eyes different than our worth in the world's eyes?

4. Do you believe your value and worth doesn't rise and fall with your performance? Why or why not?

WRAP UP

In Genesis 1, we read about how God went all in as the Creator. Over the course of six days, He created the heavens and the earth (v. 1), separated the light from the darkness (v. 2), separated the water from the sky (v. 6), created dry land (v. 9), produced vegetation of all kinds (v. 11), created the sun, moon and stars (vv. 14-17), and filled the oceans and the earth with every kind of bird, fish and animal creature (vv. 20-26).

But even after putting every ounce of His divine creativity into planet Earth, God saved His most prized creation for last—He first formed man out of the dust and breathed life into him (Genesis 2:7). Not wanting man to be alone, God took a rib from his body and created the first woman (Genesis 2:21-22). God's great love for mankind is the source of everyone's self-worth.

God's creative plan from the very beginning contained these key points:

- **God's Love Is All In.** God created you because He loved you. Even before you were born, He loved you and desired a relationship with you. Read John 15:15 and 1 John 4:19.
- **God's Sacrifice Is All In**. After man sinned, God prepared the ultimate sacrifice—the life of His only son Jesus—to die in our place and give us the opportunity to have eternal life. Read John 3:16.
- **God's Purpose Is All In.** God created you for a purpose. He wants you to be a part of His great plan! Read Jeremiah 29:11 and Ephesians 2:10.

Allow me to expand on the four words "God is for us" found in Romans 8:31. He is ahead of us, leading the way. He is alongside us, standing with us in every situation. He is behind us, our greatest fan. He is under us, providing a sure foundation. He is above us, watching over every move. He is inside us, empowering us to live for Him. God says, "You are worth it." You want proof? God sent His Son to die for you. God is for you! Live confidently and courageously in light of this truth.

1. Write down and then openly share your thoughts on how you view yourself, how you perceive others view you, and how you perceive God views you.

2. What are some negative views you have about yourself or negative views you perceive your teammates and/or God might have of you? What do you think is the source of those negative views?

3. In which of these ways has God already revealed to you He is 'all in'? In which of these areas have you struggled to believe God is 'all in'? How do these scriptures encourage you to receive God's 'all-in' love, sacrifice, and purpose?

4. Respond to this statement. "Your worth does not increase or decrease based on what others might say or think of you. Your worth comes from God who made you and saved you."

COACHING CONNECTION

In your role as a coach, how does it make you feel to know God is for you? Your worth as a coach is extremely valuable because God has said you are worth it.

God went all in to demonstrate your true value. He created this world for you. He lovingly created you and even had you in mind before you were conceived. God showed the ultimate act of going all in by sending His only Son, Jesus to die on the Cross for your sin, but God didn't stop there. He also created you for a purpose. He saw the future and provided a way for you to serve Him and bring glory to His name. You will never truly understand your total worth until you accept the gift of salvation God has made available to you.

Character Attributes Survey

This survey is intended to help you and your team assess personal and team character attributes. The results can be analyzed by you individually for your personal growth, but analyzing your team's collective responses can also provide an overview of the areas your team is strong, along with areas for growth.

INSTRUCTIONS: For each item below, circle the number that most closely reflects your personal sense of the strength or weakness of the given character attribute in your own life.

SCALE

1   2   3   4   5   6   7   8   9   10

WEAK   **STRONG**

1. Love: I easily develop deep personal attachments and affection for other people.

1   2   3   4   5   6   7   8   9   10

2. Big: I believe God has something of great significance for me to accomplish in my limited time here on earth.

1   2   3   4   5   6   7   8   9   10

3. Blessing: I eagerly embrace opportunities to invoke favor and honor upon others.

1   2   3   4   5   6   7   8   9   10

4. Breadth: I display depth and broadness, in my words and deeds, within my heart and mind.

1   2   3   4   5   6   7   8   9   10

5. Family: I understand the need to choose family over isolation by being part of something bigger than myself.

1   2   3   4   5   6   7   8   9   10

6. Fear: I constantly battle unpleasant emotions brought on by dangerous, painful or threatening situations.

1   2   3   4   5   6   7   8   9   10

7. Forgiveness: I am able to clear the record of those who have wronged me and not hold their past offenses against them.

     1   2   3   4   5   6   7   8   9   10

8. Hate: I find myself having an intense and passionate dislike for specific people or specific actions.

     1   2   3   4   5   6   7   8   9   10

9. Hospitality: I cheerfully share food, shelter and my life with those with whom I come in contact.

     1   2   3   4   5   6   7   8   9   10

10. Pain: I regularly experience distress, anguish and misery personally and with others due to something I have done.

     1   2   3   4   5   6   7   8   9   10

11. Passion: I often have intense, powerful or compelling emotions and feelings toward others or something

     1   2   3   4   5   6   7   8   9   10

12. Purity: I am committed to sexual purity before and after I get married.

     1   2   3   4   5   6   7   8   9   10

13. Resurrection: I believe something that is dead can become alive.

     1   2   3   4   5   6   7   8   9   10

14. Trust: It is my nature to believe totally and completely in someone or something.

     1   2   3   4   5   6   7   8   9   10

15. Truth: I am a pursuer of accurate and documented facts.

     1   2   3   4   5   6   7   8   9   10

16. Worth: I know I have great value and importance in the eyes of God Almighty.

     1   2   3   4   5   6   7   8   9   10

LOVE

GOD PURSUES ME

Opening Story

[Tell the story about Gale Sayers and Brian Piccolo (pg. 9) or another story about love.]

Chapel Points

• Love is having a deep personal attachment and affection for another person.

[Revisit the story about Brittany Viola (pg. 10) as an athlete who overcame a number of serious highs and lows, until finally coming to an understanding of how much God loved her. If you didn't use this story, use another example of a team, an athlete or coach who has shown love.]

• God is love. How have you seen God's love for you?

[Read Psalm 139:13-16.] Why is God's love for people a foundational truth?

• Share Zacchaeus' story from Luke 19:1-10. How did Jesus' love for Zacchaeus impact him? Why do you believe Zacchaeus went to such lengths to see Jesus? Why did Zacchaeus radically change his ways after his encounter with Jesus?

• Read and comment on the three bullet points and the Scripture which accompanies each point from pg. 11—God's unconditional love; God loves everyone; and God's love is forever. Why are these love statements so important for you to hear continually?

• Read and review John 3:16-17 and Romans 5:8. Why did Jesus have to die on the cross in order to pay the penalty for the sin of all mankind? What role did love play in Jesus' decision to die for your sin?

Closing Thoughts

[Recap God's love story as found in "The Four," beginning on pg. 100.]

• What would it look like for you to exhibit love as an athlete?

• Do your teammates and coaches consider you to be loving? Starting today, what would it take for you to demonstrate love to God and others?

• Love is valuing the life of someone else above your own life. Choosing to love is dying to my self-interests and instead valuing the needs of others.

Prayer

[Read this closing prayer or come up with a prayer on your own.]

Jesus, help us to love You first, and secondarily, my teammates and coaches. Help us to set aside our selfish tendencies. Use me to be a person who will love others deeply, before thinking about myself. In Your name, I pray. Amen.

BIG

GO BIG OR GO HOME

Opening Story

[Describe in your own words what it means to 'go big or go home.' (pg. 13). Share a personal experience where you attempted something outlandish. What was the result of your big dream?]

Chapel Points

• Big is possessing something of great significance.

[Prior to attempting your big dream, what mindset did you have about the possibilities of this becoming a reality? Obviously, you may not fully see the completion of your big dream but what guiding principles are true when it comes to believing in the improbable?]

• When Jim Caviezel launched his acting career, his big dream was to land a role on a soap opera. What propelled Jim to 'go big?' What would have happened to Jim had he not been convinced God had bigger plans for him?

• Jesus is in the business of doing the improbable as evidenced by the miracles He performed and the words He proclaimed. [Read Matthew 8:24-27. What did the disciples learn about Jesus from this night on the boat? How did their perspective change about Jesus going forward from this experience?]

• How did the words and life of Jesus impact the disciples? [Elaborate on Matthew 8:24-27 or share another example from Scripture where Jesus got their full attention.]

–Discuss the impact of the statements (pg. 15-16): God's love, power and purpose is big. How does the bigness of God alter your current situation?

–What kind of big power is unleashed when you believe these truths?

Closing Thoughts

[Read John 14:6; Ephesians 2:8-9 and Colossians 1:11.]

• What are big dreams you have that will make an eternal impact?

• What are steps you can take today to fulfill God's call on your life?

• How can you bring glory to God by trusting Him for the improbable?

Prayer

[Read this closing prayer or come up with a prayer on your own.]

Jesus, help us to believe anything is possible with You. You are all-knowing, all-powerful and all-present. I trust Your power, plans and purposes. As Your plans and purposes take place, allow me to bring glory, honor and praise to Your name. May people recognize Your power. Amen.

BLESSING

INVOKING FAVOR AND HONOR

Opening Story

[Share one of the stories from the documentary *Show Me The Father* (pg. 17) or another story about the father's blessing.]

Chapel Points

• Blessing is invoking favor and honor upon another person.

[Share the amazing father story of Deland McCullough as an example of an athlete who grew up without a father figure in his home, and yet Sherman Smith filled this role in an unexpected way. If you didn't use Deland's story, can you find another example of an athlete or coach who received a father's blessing?]

• Read Genesis 12:2. Why was the blessing viewed so favorably upon Abraham and future generations?

–Describe the stolen blessing story between Esau and Jacob (Genesis 25). What impact did it have on their relationship with the father and their future children?

–Read Exodus 20:5; 34:7, Numbers 14:18, and Deuteronomy 5:9. What do these verses tell us about a father's blessing?

[Summarize the story of Uzziah and the progression of generational bondage and generational sin extending to the fourth generation from 2nd Chronicles 26-28.]

• Discuss what it means to have a 'father wound?' Consider sharing your own story if it involves abuse, abandonment, lack of affirmation, distrust, or performance-based love as a way to build a bridge to others who may think they are alone.

–Read Proverbs 20:7. Review the five elements of giving a powerful blessing according to Dr. John Trent. Why are these elements so vital to a blessing?

Closing Thoughts

• If you received a father's blessing, share when and how it happened.

• If you've never received a blessing, would you consider having one today?

Prayer

[Read this closing prayer or come up with a prayer on your own.]

Jesus, I want to be blessed by You as my heavenly Father, and to also receive a father's blessing. Show me how I can experience this type of blessing right now. Use this blessing to not only heal past wounds, but fully live in Your power. Amen.

BREADTH

HEART ISSUES

Opening Story

[Share Carl Joseph's remarkable story (pg. 21-22) or another story that illustrates breadth.]

Chapel Points

• Breadth is having depth and broadness, in words and deeds, within the heart and mind.

[Today's Workout is going to focus on what is deep within the human heart. Share why your heart condition is so important when it comes to your daily relationship with God.]

• The Apostle Paul and Jesus Christ are two extraordinary biblical examples of men who displayed breadth.

[Read Paul's mindset in 2 Corinthians 4:8-9 and Charles Jefferson's statement about Jesus (pg. 22). What do you know about Paul's and Jesus' breadth based on the totality of their lives?]

• Jerry Bridges gives a thorough description of the heart (pg. 23). Discuss the four different components of the heart and the role it plays in your success, individually and on a team.

• Read various translations of Proverbs 4:23. Why does God care so much about the heart? Comment on Proverbs 21:2 and the quote shared by John Eldridge (pg.

23). Why is guarding your heart critical for every believer?

–Review the six keys to having a complete heart (pg. 24). Do you see a deepening progression as you consider each point? How does each point build upon the previous one?

–Are you fully engaged with your heart or are you just going through the motions? How can you tell the difference?

Closing Thoughts

[Read and illustrate Jeremiah 29:13; 1 Samuel 16:7; and Acts 13:22.]

• God is able to get a full understanding of each person's heart. How does this make you feel?

• React to this statement. "God isn't looking for perfection, He's looking for direction." Why is this a true statement?

Prayer

[Read this closing prayer or come up with a prayer on your own.]

Jesus, help me to pursue breadth in the way I live my day-to-day life. I desire to have a heart that beats solely for You. I commit to focusing on having a soft and responsive heart to Your ways and Your will. Help me to push away inconsistent attitudes, behavior, and conduct. Purge even the good to pursue Your best. Amen.

FAMILY

BETTER TOGETHER

Opening Story

[Tell a story about a coach or an athlete who understands the importance of family.]

Chapel Points

• Family is being part of something bigger than yourself.

[Describe your family. Discuss the impact of your parents, grandparents, aunts/uncles, cousins, and siblings on your life. Was it a healthy Christian home, or perhaps the exact opposite? How did your family shape who you are as a person right now? If married and perhaps with kids of your own, how did your upbringing contribute to your family?]

• What are some things that bond a family together?

[Tell the story of Mark 2:1-12 and how these four men literally become family to this paralyzed man.]

• Why were these four men so committed to getting their friend in front of Jesus?

–Discuss the special bond that existed among these men and the obstacles they probably encountered even on this special day.

–Share a time when you worked together with your family (or teammates) to ac-complish something bigger than yourself. What was the end result of this effort?

• Discuss and explain the three biblical principles (pg. 27) that aid all families. What can you learn from each of these principles?

Closing Thoughts

[Read Proverbs 27:17; Matthew 18:20 and Romans 12:4-5. What are each of these verses telling you about family?]

• Do you have a strong Christian family, team, or support system in place? If not, what could you proactively do to connect with like-minded people who will lock arms with you and help you to live like Him and for Him?

• How could your current family situation grow even stronger?

Prayer

[Read this closing prayer or come up with a prayer on your own.]

Jesus, I don't want to live in isolation because I know there are many things I can't handle without the help of a strong family and community of believers. Help me, Lord, to depend on You, and to be a contributor to a healthy family. I pray this in the name of Jesus Christ my Savior and Lord. Amen.

FEAR

LOVE OVERCOMES FEAR

Opening Story

[Tell the story about one or more of your fears. Has this fear stopped you from doing something you know God wants you to do? If not, how did you overcome your fear?]

Chapel Points

• Fear is having unpleasant emotions brought on by dangerous, painful or threatening situations.

[Share one, two or all three stories (pg. 30) as examples of how loving relationships played a role in helping each of these athletes overcome their fears and achieve great things. If you don't use any of these stories, share another example of an athlete or coach who overcame their fear through the power of love.]

• [Read 1 John 4:18-19 and the thoughts shared at the bottom of page 30.]

–Why are these words so important in addressing our fears?

–How does the love of Christ help in removing fear?

[Re-cap the story of the Prodigal Son and the Loving Father as found in Luke 15:11-32 (pg. 31).]

• Why is the father the hero of this story? What can we learn from both sons in this story related to both fear and love?

• Review the two key points (pg. 32). How can remembering these truths help you go forward when you are fearful?

Closing Thoughts

[Read Deuteronomy 31:6; Joshua 1:9; Isaiah 40:10 and Psalm 56:3-4. What do these verses tell you?]

• Do you live in constant fear? How have your fears stopped you from experiencing a full and abundant life?

• How does a loving Father help you in overcoming fear?

Prayer

[Read this closing prayer or come up with a prayer on your own.]

Jesus, help us not to live fearfully. Remind me of how perfect love casts out all fear. Thank You for Your divine love, which was displayed by Your obedience in going to the cross to pay the penalty for my sins. Give me the courage and determination to set aside my fears and focus on Your love. Reign and rule in my life. For Your glory. Amen.

FORGIVENESS
HAPPINESS = FORGIVING EASILY

Opening Story

[Tell the Chris Webber story (pg. 33) story or another story about a major mistake you or another person made which needed forgiveness.]

Chapel Points

• Forgiveness is clearing the record of those who have wronged me and not holding their past offenses against them.

[Use Barney Sarver's example (pg. 34) or another athlete or a coach as an example of a person who chose forgiveness.]

• Read Ephesians 4:31-32, Colossians 3:12-13 and Matthew 6:14-15. God is commanding us to forgive. Why is forgiving others so important?

[Read the parable of the unforgiving servant (Matthew 18:21-35). What are the lessons we can learn from this parable?]

• Which is easier—to forgive someone for the wrong they have done to you or to seek forgiveness from someone you have offended?

–Why are both of these difficult?

–Why are both of these so important?

• Review Luke 22:54-62 and Matthew 26:57-75. As noted in these passages,

Peter blew it multiple times. How do you think Peter responded when the Lord still believed in him after these mistakes? What are the keys to forgiveness?

Closing Thoughts

[Read Mark 11:25. How does praying and forgiving others tie together?]

• Is there someone you need to forgive? Is there someone who needs to forgive you? What steps are necessary for either of these situations to take place?

• The choice is yours. Forgiveness is a decision. And when you choose forgiveness, "God will forgive you."

Prayer

[Read this closing prayer or come up with a prayer on your own.]

God, I'm commanded to forgive, and until I do so, You say in Your Word, I'm not forgiven. No matter how difficult it may be to forgive, today I choose forgiveness. Thank You, Lord, for forgiving me and believing in me, even when I frequently blow it. I'm overwhelmingly grateful. Amen.

HATE

LOVE OBLITERATES HATE

Opening Story

[Tell the Alexander Mattison story and the subsequent response by the NFL, NFLPA, and the Minnesota Vikings (pg. 37) or another story illustrating hate.]

Chapel Points

• Hate is an intense and passionate dislike for someone or something.

[Share a personal story on how you have witnessed hatred or hate speech. How has this personally affected you and your community? How do you believe God views hate?]

• The Bible has a lot to say about hate. In fact, there are things the Bible says we are to hate, and there are also things we are not supposed to hate. Do a Scripture search on 'hate' and share what you learned.

[In addition to what you found in your Scripture search, also read Malachi 2:16; Luke 14:26; Luke 6:27-38; Galatians 6:7; 1 John 4:7-21 and 1 Peter 1:22.]

• Is hating sinful? What are some of the takeaways from these passages related to 'hate'?

–How does unconditional love obliterate hate?

–How does sowing and reaping change the way you view hate?

• Share the North Korean POW story and the four primary hate tactics implemented. Why were these hate tactics so successful?

Closing Thoughts

[Read Proverbs 18:1.]

• How do our words bring life or death to others?

• Why do the words "I love you" or "I hate you" create powerful emotional responses?

• How can you lead with love?

Prayer

[Read this closing prayer or come up with a prayer on your own.]

Jesus, I want to be known as a person who loves and doesn't hate. I invite You to be in control of my thoughts, attitudes, and behaviors because what is going through my mind will eventually come out of my mouth. May the words I share reflect Your love. Help me to follow You faithfully every single minute, hour and day. I love You. Amen.

HOSPITALITY

BEARING ONE ANOTHER'S BURDENS

Opening Story

[Tell a story involving a church or non-profit in your area that helps provide food, shelter, or clothing to people in need in your community. In addition, share the amazing story of Tori Murden (pages 41 and 42) and how her hospitality helped one of her primary competitors.]

Chapel Points

• Hospitality is cheerfully sharing food, shelter and my life with others.

[Hospitality opportunities are available pretty much every day and in every community. There are people who need something which you can offer to them.]

• What are the various needs people have in your city and community?

• Who are some of the people providing resources and help to those in need? How are you personally involved in any of these situations?

[Tell the story of the Acts 2:42–47 church and what they did to respond to those in need.]

• How did the people respond to those who showed them hospitality?

–What was the impact of their Galatians 6:2 mindset?

–Why did the Acts 2 church see such a rapid growth in their numbers?

• How does genuinely caring for and meeting the needs of others impact others? Consider the story of Douglas MacArthur in your response.

Closing Thoughts

[Read Matthew 5:13-16 and the other verses shared on pg. 44.]

• Would people describe you as 'hospitable?' Why or why not?

• What are ways you can make people more comfortable or help take your relationship to a deeper level?

• When you show hospitality, what should you expect in return?

Prayer

[Read this closing prayer or come up with a prayer on your own.]

Jesus, help me to express the gift of hospitality in the same way You would do so. I desire to be living proof of a loving God to a watching world. This kind of active love is one way I can express my incredible thanks to You. I love You Lord. Amen.

CHAPEL OUTLINE
PAIN
HESED IS THE PAINKILLER

Opening Story

[Tell the scandalous story about Dave Bliss and the pain that resulted (pg. 45) or another story about an athlete or coach who caused pain to themselves and/or others.]

Chapel Points

• Pain is experiencing distress, anguish and misery for myself and possibly others through something that has happened.

[Physical, emotional, mental and spiritual pain is a part of every human's life. No one is exempt from pain. In this Workout, we will learn God's faithful love, known as 'hesed,' is at the core of God's love story.]

• What was Jesus' mission?

[Review John 19 and what was happening with Jesus before and after His death on the cross.]

• Why did Jesus have to go to the cross and endure the pain He experienced?

–How did the two criminals on each side of Jesus react and respond to Jesus?

–How does it make you feel knowing 'the man on the middle cross said I can come?'

• The death of Jesus wasn't the end—it was the beginning. Why is this true?

• Discuss God's three incredible responses to the hopelessness and despair that sin and pain bring to our lives (pg. 47). How does His pain help you with your pain?

Closing Thoughts

[Read Romans 5:8; Psalm 147:3 and Romans 8:28.]

• How do each of these verses help us when we are in the midst of pain?

• Jesus came to earth to pay the penalty for the sin of all mankind and to restore a right relationship with His Father. Through His sacrifice, He won the ultimate victory over sin. Describe the impact of 'hesed' on your life. Why is this such an amazing word?

Prayer

[Read this closing prayer or come up with a prayer on your own.]

Jesus, thank You for embracing the pain and completing Your mission by going to the cross to pay the penalty for my sin. Only You can offer forgiveness, restoration, and healing. Again, I say thank You for Your 'hesed'!! Help me to embrace the pain that I experience daily and see it as a way to make me more Christ-like. Amen.

PASSION
LAYING IT ALL OUT FOR HIM

Opening Story

[Tell the story of Lonise Bias (pg. 49) or another story of someone who is living passionately.]

Chapel Points

• Passion is having an intense, powerful or compelling emotion and feelings toward others or something.

[It was the passion (or suffering) of Jesus that led Him to be crucified on the cross. Only the worst of the worst were crucified. Yet, what was Jesus' sin? Why was He subjected to this type of cruel death?]

• Describe what a typical Roman crucifixion involved. How did Jesus' crucifixion differ from others who experienced this same brutality?

[All four Gospels give a detailed account of the passion of Jesus. Share a brief overview of what Jesus went through beginning with His arrest in the Garden of Gethsemane.]

• The beatings, the taunts from the crowd, the gruesome walk to Calvary, and the nails driven into His hands and feet were all part of God's supreme plan to save mankind.

–Was this going to be easy for Jesus? Obviously, it is not based on Him sweat-ing drops of blood even before He was arrested (Luke 22:44). Why do you think He was bleeding even before the beatings began?

–Jesus chose to die (John 10:17-18). Why is this such a significant part of Jesus' passion?

Closing Thoughts

[Read 1 Corinthians 15:13-17.]

• Paul basically says we are all idiots, our faith is useless, and we are still guilty of our sins if Jesus didn't rise from the dead. Why is this true?

• The resurrection of Jesus is the most important event of all time, and there isn't a close second. Why is this statement true?

• How does Jesus' passion impact you to be a person of passion? What are some ways you can live with passion in your daily life?

Prayer

[Read this closing prayer or come up with a prayer on your own.]

Jesus, Your passion helps me to be a person of passion. Give me ears to hear, eyes to see, and wisdom on how to live passionately for You. This won't be easy, but it will be worth it. In Jesus' name. Amen.

PURITY

STAYING CLEAR FROM THE FILTH

Opening Story

[Tell the story about what transpired at the University of Michigan or Michigan State (pg. 53) or another inappropriate purity incident.]

Chapel Points

• Purity is freeing yourself from anything that contaminates or adulterates.

[Sex is a beautiful thing created by God, which is reserved exclusively for a man and a woman who are married. All sexual activity outside of this standard is sexual misconduct.]

• Purity is hard; impurity is easy.

[Recap Ezra 9:1-15 and 10:1-17. What do we learn about purity under Ezra's leadership?]

• God's Word challenges us to pursue purity. Read Romans 13:14; 1 Corinthians 6:18 and Hebrews 13:4.

–Why should we not gratify the desires of our sinful nature?

–How is fleeing sexual immorality an excellent strategy for remaining pure?

–Why does God's judgment come upon those who are living impure lives?

• Living by God's standard of purity brings deep joy and real sexual satisfaction.

Closing Thoughts

[Read some or all of the Scripture passages noted on pg. 55-56.]

• Do you believe it is possible to live a pure life in an impure world?

• Review the quotes stated by Jerry Kirk and Randy Alcorn throughout this Workout. Why are these statements true?

• What are the keys to remaining pure?

Prayer

[Read this closing prayer or come up with a prayer on your own.]

Jesus, living a pure life in an impure world is going to require me to be strong in the Lord. It appears our sex-crazed culture goes against everything You say about purity in Your Word. I humbly come before You, asking for You to help me keep my eyes on the prize that awaits me. All I have to do is cry out for help, and You will be there to aid me every step of the way. Do the work Lord Jesus! Amen..

RESURRECTION
LIAR, LUNATIC, OR LORD

Opening Story

[Tell the backstory behind the Tommy John surgery (pg. 57) and how this surgery has resurrected thousands of careers over the past 50 years.]

Chapel Points

• Resurrection is miraculously witnessing someone or something coming back to life after it is pronounced dead.

[The resurrection of Jesus Christ is the single most important event in the history of mankind. If Christ didn't rise from the dead, Paul says our faith is useless, and we are to be pitied. Read 1 Corinthians 15:1-34. Why did Paul believe in the resurrection? What happens to Paul and all of us if the resurrection didn't happen?]

• There are a number of conspiracy theories abounding about what could have happened to the body of Jesus when it was missing on the third day after His crucifixion. Discuss these theories (the disciples stole the dead body, Jesus didn't really die, the witnesses went to the wrong grave, etc.). Why do each of these theories fall apart upon investigation?

[Read Matthew 28 and John 20:24-29.]

• Why is Thomas' testimony so compelling?

–Why are the post-resurrection actions of the disciples such an important part of believing Jesus truly did rise from the dead?

–Why does the Chuck Colson quote (pg. 58) give credence to the resurrection?

Closing Thoughts

[Read Romans 1:4 and 4:25.]

• How does the death, burial and resurrection of Jesus Christ, more than 2,000 years ago, personally impact you today?

• Liar, Lunatic or Lord. Jesus can only be one of these three. Why is this true, and what are the ramifications if He truly is the Lord?

Prayer

[Read this closing prayer or come up with a prayer on your own.]

Jesus, I believe You rose from the dead. The evidence is clear. Every conspiracy theory has major gaps. The only thing that makes sense is Your resurrection. Like Paul, I believe the facts, and I embrace You as the King of Kings and the Lord of Lords. I worship and bow down to You all the days of my life. Amen.

TRUST

TRUST BEGINS WITH CHRIST

Opening Story

[Tell the story about Jim Marshall (pg. 61), who, after an infamous mistake, later became someone his teammates could count on. If you don't use this story, share one about someone you trust.]

Chapel Points

• Trust is believing completely and totally in someone or something.

[The Team Builder exercise is a "must do" experience to fully understand this Workout. Therefore, at a minimum, do this activity with a partner and share what you learned from this experience with the entire group.]

[Read Matthew 14:22-33. What does this story tell us about trust?]

• Peter jumped out of the boat and began walking on the water toward Jesus. Why? What happened when he stopped looking at Jesus?

–Peter knew Jesus was a man of integrity. Jesus commanded him to come, and Peter believed Him.

–Peter knew Jesus loved him deeply. He knew Jesus would not let him down.

[Read some or all of Acts 9:1-22.]

• Saul's Damascus road experience altered his life dramatically. Why did Saul trust in this moment?

• Ananias was well aware of Saul's background. Why did he trust God when asked him to go be with Saul?

Closing Thoughts

[Read Proverbs 27:6.]

• Share the benefits of having trustworthy friends in your life.

• Who are some of the people you can trust? Why did you select them?

• Trust is the glue of all relationships. Why is this true?

Prayer

[Read this closing prayer or come up with a prayer on your own.]

Jesus, just like You called Peter to walk on the water, You are calling me to trust You as well. Today, I jump out of the boat and fix my eyes solely on You. I give all I have to You. Amen.

.

TRUTH

TRUTH ALWAYS BEATS LIES

Opening Story

[Tell the story about Kelly Clark (pg. 66) or another story about believing the truth.]

Chapel Points

• Truth is believing accurate and documented facts.

[Revisit the story about Kelly Clark and why her success in her sport radically changed after she realized "who she was and whose she was."]

• When people have a proper view of themselves (who they are) and of God (whose they are), they are now living in truth. Why is understanding our identity so important?

[Tell the story of Eve and the serpent in the Garden of Eden (Genesis 3:1–7). How did the serpent's lying words "Did God really say…" trip her up?]

• Review the truth points and related Scripture shared on page 67.

–Which one(s) have impacted your athletic career?

–Which one(s) have impacted your non-athletic career?

• Read Matthew 4:1–11. How did Jesus combat the devil's lies?

• Where are you right now? Are you listening to God's truth or the devil's lies? Are you ready for God to direct you? Where do you want to be? What are your goals, dreams, and aspirations?

Closing Thoughts

[Read Jeremiah 29:11.]

• Do you believe God has a wonderful plan for your life? If so, share it.

• What lies do you need to stop believing?

• Reflect on the truths God has given to you. How does living in the truth feel to you on a daily basis?

Prayer

[Read this closing prayer or come up with a prayer on your own.]

Jesus, when You were tempted in the wilderness by the devil in Matthew 4, You countered every lie by sharing the truth from God's Word. Lord, help me to be devoted to studying and memorizing God's Word so that when the lies come, I will be able to respond with Your truth. With every fiber of my body, I commit to being a person of truth. For Your glory. Amen.

CHAPEL OUTLINE
WORTH
GOD IS ALL IN

Opening Story

[Tell the story about Jackie Robinson and Branch Rickey (pg. 70) or another person seeking worth.]

Chapel Points

• Worth has great value and importance.

[Both Robinson and Rickey had to be 'all in' to face the racial battle that was boiling in America at the time. If either one of them wavered, it could have been a major setback. Their 'all in' spirit demonstrated value and importance. Share both current and Bible examples of men and women who also have an 'all in' mentality.]

• God is the initiator of our worth, as evidenced by what He has done for us through His love, sacrifice and purpose (pg. 71).

[Read Genesis 1:1-26. How does the creation story reveal what God values?]

• God is for us (Romans 8:31). Dissect the statement made on page 72. Why is this such a motivating statement?

• God says, "You are worth it." How does this make you feel?

–He created you in your mother's womb to accomplish great and mighty things. He is the giver and sustainer of life.

–He is faithful. He keeps all of His promises.

–He can be trusted. He will never let you down.

–He loves you. His Son is evidence of this fact (John 3:16).

Closing Thoughts

[Read Psalm 139:13-16.]

• Who knows you better than anyone else?

• Why does having value and importance bring energy to your dreams?

• How can you grow in deeper intimacy with your Heavenly Father?

Prayer

[Read this closing prayer or come up with a prayer on your own.]

Jesus, thank You for valuing me and reminding me of how important I am to You. You went to the cross, which is a clear sign of how much You believe in me. Help me to stay faithfully devoted to Your ways and Your Word. Allow me to experience You to the fullest. Amen.

STEP UP TO LIFE

by Elmer Murdoch

On the following pages you're going to see that there
are five, distinct "steps" that mark out an athlete's spiritual journey.
You'll be able to look at these and self-diagnose exactly where you
are in your journey. The following steps are like a spiritual GPS /
mapping system, allowing you to measure your spiritual progress.

These steps define the attitude of a person's heart towards God,
NOT how much they know about God, Jesus Christ
or the Gospel. Those are issues of the head.
The steps take you into the heart.

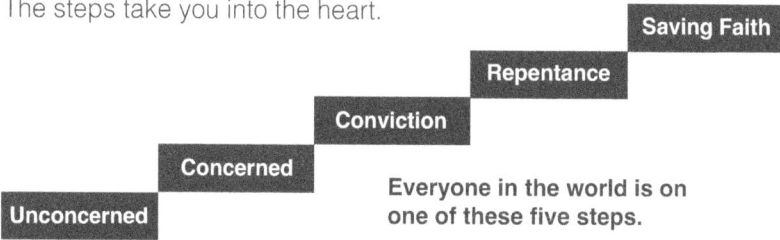

Saving Faith

Repentance

Conviction

Concerned

Unconcerned

**Everyone in the world is on
one of these five steps.**

What spiritual step are you on?
Discover that, and then see what the next step is that God has for
you. Then you can move forward from there.

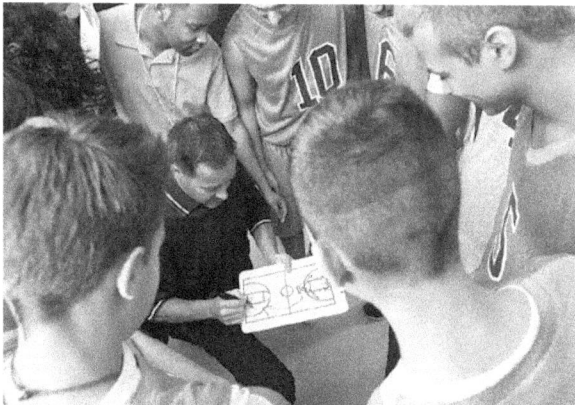

You can read about these five steps in the story Jesus told about the Prodigal Son in Luke 15:11-24. The rebellious son clearly starts on the first step of Unconcerned but, at the end of the parable, clearly ends on the top step of Saving Faith...he was "dead" but now is "alive." He was "lost" but now is "found."

2. Concerned

1. Unconcerned

All athletes start right here. You may KNOW a lot about Jesus and the gospel or very little. You may even respect Him. But, unconcerned athletes don't really care about a personal relationship with Him.

Athletes on this step sense emptiness, dissatisfaction or even fear. You know there is more to life than what you're experiencing. What's life about? Why am I here? You've been awakened to your spiritual need.

The first question God ever asked a human being was, "Where are you (Adam and Eve)?" It's still a great question for today. Where are you in your spiritual journey? Look carefully at the following pages, studying the steps and discover exactly where you are.

4. Repentance

3. Conviction

These athletes are feeling guilt and a type of spiritual discomfort and emptiness. Selfish, "please me" choices are sinful and break God's Ten Commandments. God's passing grade on goodness is keeping the 10 Commandments perfectly in thought, word and deed. You have failed and you're feeling bothered.

Athletes here are ready to make a spiritual U-turn... where YOU turn. You turn from running your own life apart from Jesus Christ and turn TO Him. "Self" is dethroned in your heart, making room for Christ to be enthroned. Head Athlete Jesus said, "Unless you repent, you will all perish." *Luke 13:3*

5. Saving Faith

Athletes on this step are all in. They've given Jesus Christ their whole life and the right to run it. They've surrendered to the total rule of Jesus in their lives. He is the head coach, calling all the plays. Christ's death is the payment for your sins. God receives you as His child and puts His very life right inside of you. "If you confess with your mouth Jesus is Lord and believe in your heart that God raised Him from the dead, you will be saved."

Where Are You?

Unconcerned
___ I don't really care.

Concerned
___ I'm concerned.

Conviction
___ I cheated and am guilty.

Repentance
___ I'm making a U-turn, I'm doing a complete "180."

Saving Faith
___ I'm all in and making Jesus my Lord and Savior today.

Therefore:
___ I am confessing my sins to God. *I John 1:9*
___ I am turning from and repenting of my sin. *Acts 17:30*
___ I am putting my faith in the Lord Jesus and thanking Him for His Life in me. *Romans 8:16*

www.stepuptolife.com

more than

Winning

discovering
GOD'S PLAN FOR YOUR LIFE

God's Plan

In most athletic contests, a coach prepares a game plan ahead of time. God designed a plan for our lives before the world began.

God is holy and perfect. He created us to love Him, glorify Him, and enjoy Him forever.

WHAT IS GOD'S STANDARD?

The Bible, God's playbook, says that the standard for being on His team is to:

Be holy.
 "Be holy, because I am holy." - I Peter 1:16b

Be perfect.
 "Be perfect, therefore, as your heavenly Father is perfect." - Matthew 5:48

WHAT IS GOD'S PLAN?

God created us to:

Love Him.
 "Jesus replied: 'Love the Lord your God with all your heart and with all your soul and with all your mind.' " - Matthew 22:37

Glorify (honor) Him.
 "You are worthy, our Lord and God, to receive glory and honor and power, for you created all things, and by your will they were created and have their being." - Revelation 4:11

Enjoy Him forever.
 Jesus said, "...I have come that they may have life, and have it to the full." - John 10:10b

Why is it we cannot live up to God's standard of holiness and perfection? Because of...

Man's Problem

Man is sinful and separated from God.

WHAT IS SIN?

Sin means missing the mark, falling short of God's standard. It is not only doing wrong and failing to do what God wants (lying, gossip, losing our temper, lustful thoughts, etc.), it is also an attitude of ignoring or rejecting God, which is a result of our sinful nature.

"Surely I was sinful at birth, sinful from the time my mother conceived me." - Psalm 51:5

WHO HAS SINNED?

"For all have sinned and fall short of the glory of God." - Romans 3:23

WHAT ARE THE RESULTS OF SIN?

Separation from God.
"But your iniquities [sins] have separated you from your God..." - Isaiah 59:2a
Death.
"For the wages of sin is death..." - Romans 6:23
Judgment.
"Just as man is destined to die once, and after that to face judgment..." - Hebrews 9:27

This illustration shows that God is holy and we are sinful and separated from Him. Man continually tries to reach God through his own efforts (being good, religious activities, philosophy, etc.) but, while these can be good things, they all fall short of God's standard.
"...all our righteous acts [good works] are like filthy rags." - Isaiah 64:6b

There is only one way to bridge this gap between God and man. We need...

God's Substitute

God provided the only way to be on His team by sending His Son, Jesus Christ, as the holy and perfect substitute to die in our place.

WHO IS JESUS CHRIST?

He is God.
Jesus said, "I and the Father are one." - John 10:30

He is Man.
"...the Word (Jesus) was God...The Word became flesh and made his dwelling among us." - John 1:1,14a

WHAT HAS JESUS DONE?

He died as our substitute.
"...God demonstrates his own love for us in this: While we were still sinners, Christ died for us." - Romans 5:8

He rose from the dead.
"...Christ died for our sins...he was buried...he was raised on the third day according to the Scriptures, and ...he appeared to Peter, and then to the Twelve. After that, he appeared to more than five hundred..." - 1 Corinthians 15:3-6

He is the only way to God.
"...I am the way and the truth and the life. No one comes to the Father except through me." - John 14:6

This illustration shows that God has bridged the gap between Himself and man by sending Jesus Christ to die in our place as our substitute. Jesus defeated sin and death and rose from the grave. Yet, it isn't enough just to know these facts. To become a part of God's team, there must be...

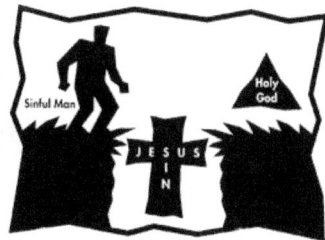

Man's Response

Knowing a lot about a sport and "talking the game" doesn't make you a member of a team. The same is true in becoming a Christian. It takes more than just knowing about Jesus Christ; it requires a total commitment by faith in Him.

FAITH IS NOT:

Just knowing the facts.
"You believe that there is one God. Good! Even the demons believe that – and shudder."
- James 2:19

Just an emotional experience.
Raising your hand or repeating a prayer is not enough.

FAITH IS:

Repenting.
Turning to God from sin.
"Godly sorrow brings repentance that leads to salvation and leaves no regret..."
- 2 Corinthians 7:10a

Receiving Jesus Christ.
Trusting in Christ alone for salvation.
"Yet to all who received him, to those who believed in his name, he gave the right to become children of God..." *- John 1:12*

On which side of the illustration do you see yourself? Where would you like to be?

Jesus said, "I tell you the truth, whoever hears my word and believes him who sent me has eternal life and will not be condemned; he has crossed over from death to life." - John 5:24

To make sure we are making the right call, let's look at the...

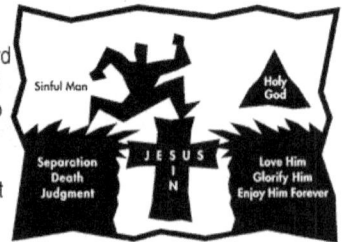

Replay of God's Plan

- **REALIZE** God is holy and perfect; we are sinners and cannot save ourselves.
- **RECOGNIZE** who Jesus is and what He's done as our substitute.
- **REPENT** by turning to God from sin.
- **RECEIVE** Jesus Christ by faith as Savior and Lord.
- **RESPOND** to Jesus Christ in a life of obedience.

Jesus said, "...If anyone would come after me, he must deny himself and take up his cross daily and follow me." - Luke 9:23

Does God's plan make sense to you? Are you willing to repent and receive Jesus Christ? If so, express to God your need for Him. If you're not sure what to say, consider the "Suggested Prayer of Commitment" below. Remember that God is more concerned with your attitude than with the words you say.

SUGGESTED PRAYER OF COMMITMENT:

"Lord Jesus, I need you. I realize I'm a sinner, and I can't save myself. I need your mercy. I believe that you died on the cross for my sins and rose from the dead. I repent of my sins and put my faith in you as Savior and Lord. Take control of my life, and help me to follow you in obedience. In Jesus' name. Amen."

"...If you confess with your mouth, 'Jesus is Lord,' and believe in your heart that God raised him from the dead, you will be saved. ... for, 'Everyone who calls on the name of the Lord will be saved.'" - Romans 10:9,13

Once you have committed your life to Jesus Christ, it is important for you to...

Point 1 / God Loves You

God made you and loves you! His love is boundless and unconditional. God is real, and He wants you to personally experience His love and discover the purpose of your life through a relationship with Him.

Genesis 1:27 and John 3:16

Point 2 / Sin Separates You

You cannot experience God's love when you ignore Him. People search everywhere for meaning and fulfillment—but not with God. They don't trust God and ignore His ways. The Bible calls this sin. Everyone has sinned.

Sin damages your relationships with other people and with God. The result: you are eternally separated from God and the life He planned for you.

Romans 3:23, Romans 6:23, Isaiah 59:2

Point 3 / Jesus Rescues You

Sin does not stop God from loving you. Because of God's great love, He became a human being in Jesus Christ and gave His life for you. At the cross, Jesus took your place and paid the penalty of death that you deserve for your sins.

Jesus died, but He rose to life again. Jesus offers you peace with God and a personal relationship with Him. Through faith in Jesus, you can experience God's love daily, discover your purpose and have eternal life after death.

1 Peter 3:18, 1 Corinthians 15:3-8, Romans 5:8

Point 4 / Will you trust jesus?

God has already done everything to show you how much He loves you. He offers you fulfillment and eternal life through a relationship with Jesus Christ. This involves agreeing that you are sinful, accepting God's forgiveness and turning away from your sins and toward God.

You choose to trust Jesus when you believe and confess that Jesus is Lord and surrender your life to Him. Are you ready to place your trust in Jesus?

Finding Love in Sports: THE FELLOWSHIP OF THE UNASHAMED

The greatest expression of love ever known was Jesus willingly giving up His life for us. It was the biggest sacrifice and a continual reminder that love isn't easy. Real love requires something from us. It costs us something. John 15:13 says, "There is no greater love than to lay down one's life for one's friends." Every time we make a sacrifice in the name of love, remember the sacrifice God made for all of us. Use it as motivation to keep moving in the direction of love.

Allow me to tell you about one of my heroes. I love this man and admire the love he had for the Lord. We've never met and our first face to face meeting will be in heaven when I join him. He's been there since 1980 and the crazy part of the story is I don't even know his name. Here's what I do know. He obviously loved Jesus more than anyone else or anything this life could offer him. He is known as the leader of a group of people referred to as "The Fellowship of The Unashamed."

In 1980, this man was living in Rwanda, Africa and the people in his village obviously weren't happy about his Christian faith. He was forced by his tribe to either renounce Christ or face certain death. He was not ashamed of the Gospel and the saving message of Jesus Christ. He refused to renounce Christ, and he was killed on the spot. The following day, people went to his home to remove his belongings and they found a letter he had written the night before his execution; that letter is now known around the world. It reads as follows:

I am a part of the "Fellowship of the Unashamed." I have the Holy Spirit power. The die has been cast. I have stepped over the line. The decision has been made. I am a disciple of Jesus Christ. I won't look back, let up, slow down, back away, or be still.

My past is redeemed, my present makes sense, and my future is secure. I am finished and done with low living, sight walking, small planning, smooth knees, colorless dreams, tame visions, mundane talking, chintzy giving, and dwarfed goals.

I no longer need pre-eminence, prosperity, position, promotions, plaudits, or popularity. I don't have to be right, first, tops, recognized, praise, regarded or rewarded. I now live by presence, lean by faith, love by patience, lift by prayer, and labor by power.

My pace is set, my gait is fast, my goal is Heaven, my road is narrow, my way is rough, my compassions few, my Guide reliable, my mission clear.

I cannot be bought, compromised, deterred, lured away, turned back, diluted, or delayed. I will not flinch in the face of sacrifice, hesitate in the presence of adversity, negotiate at the table of the enemy, ponder at the pool of popularity, or meander in the maze of mediocrity.

I will not give up, back up, let up or shut up until I've preached up, prayed up, paid up, stored up and stayed up for the cause of Christ.

I am a disciple of Jesus Christ. I must go until He returns, give until I drop, preach until all know, and work until He comes. And when He comes to get His own, He will have no problem recognizing me. My colors will be clear.

Notice the word 'love' is not mentioned one time in this mantra, but love oozes out of this man's heart. The Apostle Paul said in Romans 1:16, "For I am not ashamed of this Good News about Christ. It is the power of God at work, saving everyone who believes—the Jew first and also the Gentile."

I was so inspired by these words and decided to memorize them in 2019 while doing my daily pushup and plank routine. For almost six years (70+ months and counting to be exact), I recite "The Fellowship of the Unashamed" by memory at least one time daily during my planks. Often they are the first words I share when I speak at men's conferences. It has become part of my DNA. His words motivate and inspire me to love not only my Lord and Savior Jesus Christ but also to love everyone who crosses my path.

I urge you to also become a member of "The Fellowship of the Unashamed." It's all about loving Him and loving others in what today is known as "The Most Important Commandment" or "The Great Commandment." Matthew 22:36-40 says, "Teacher, which is the most important commandment in the law of Moses?" Jesus replied, "'You must love the LORD your God with all your heart, all your soul, and all your mind.' This is the first and greatest commandment. A second is equally important, 'Love your neighbor as yourself.' The entire law and all the demands of the prophets are based on these two commandments."

In closing, remember this great quote from Billy Graham, "It's God's job to judge; it's the Holy Spirit's job to convict and it's my job to love."

DOING SPORTS
GOD'S WAY

A BIBLICAL HANDBOOK
FOR COACHES AND ATHLETES

KINGDOM SPORTS

GOAL + MOTIVATION · STRATEGY · SUCCESS

GOAL

EYES ON THE RIGHT KING

1. How do you define the term "goal" as it relates to your athletic performance?

2. How often do you reach or achieve your athletic goals?

3. How do you feel when you achieve your athletic goals?

4. How do you feel when you fail to reach your athletic goals?

WHAT IS YOUR GOAL?

That's a big question that might have different answers throughout your life. Some goals are achieved quickly, perhaps even daily, while others are accomplished over months, years, or even a lifetime.

For the competitive coach or athlete, some goals might be to win a game, to win a conference, state or national championship, to set records, to earn a scholarship, or to get paid. Other goals might be to build relationships, to become stronger, to become a better person, or to impact the community with your platform.

None of those goals are inherently bad and in fact many of them are noble and commendable. But they all become improper goals if they fall into the "self-satisfying" category, and will leave you empty, hinder your performance, and hinder your maximum development.

One of the dangers of a self-satisfying goal is when things get tough (through pain, exhaustion, or failure), your natural tendency is to ease up or quit, which ironically also brings immediate satisfaction. Although you get personal recognition as a winner, you also get personal relief when you ease up or quit. Your maximum athletic development, however, is delayed in that moment.

That's why the only way to be fully satisfied as a Christian athlete or coach is to have the right goals—to glorify God, to build His Kingdom and most importantly to be totally conformed to the image of Jesus Christ (see Romans 8:29).

Conforming to the likeness of Jesus is the only goal that can release a Christian competitor's full potential. It's not a self-satisfying goal but it will help release a greater measure of ability that you already have.

The practice of focusing your attention on being in the very presence of Jesus will fill your mind with new attitudes. Jesus demonstrated this with the mindset of wanting to please His Father above everything else, which brought Him through punishing physical torment on the cross—pain that would have stopped anyone else from entering the fight in the first place.

"...for the joy set before Him endured the cross, despising the shame, and has sat down at the right hand of the throne of God." (Hebrews 12:2/ NASB)

In order to have Jesus' attitude in your athletic performance and conform to His likeness, first of all, you must have the right aim. Just like an archer focuses on the bullseye on the target, you must identify the correct spiritual goal and continually stay focused on that target.

As Jesus told His disciples, what you allow into your eyes will determine the health of your soul and your effectiveness in achieving that goal:

"Your eye is like a lamp that provides light for your body. When your eye is healthy, your whole body is filled with light. But when your eye is unhealthy, your whole body is filled with darkness. And if the light you think you have is actually darkness, how deep that darkness is!" (Matthew 6:22-23)

Once you have your eyes set on the correct aim or target, you must allow the Holy Spirit to control your thoughts and your actions. The Holy Spirit will show you from God's Word, how Jesus sized up any situation you might face.

In the Doing Sports God's Way book, it will help us examine how our Christ-likeness fits within our effort in sports. The first chapter will help us understand that before we can truly be like Jesus, we must first acknowledge the broken nature within today's sports culture and how we need a revelation that will lead us to repentance. That's our first Goal.

We will then focus on three fruits of the Holy Spirit—[Love, Faithfulness, and Self-Control]—found in Galatians 5:22-23, which will become the foundation in our goal to become conformed to Christ.

But before diving in, take some time to answer the following questions and assess what you currently believe about the intersection of athletic goals and God's call to conformity to Christ:

1. Have you ever set improper goals? If so, what was the result of doing so?

2. What is the danger of setting self-satisfying goals for your athletic performance?

3. What impact might focusing on Christ have on your athletic performance?

4. Yes or No: I believe that in sports, I am responsible to speak and act as much like Jesus as possible. (Explain your answer)

KINGDOM CONNECTION

Only one goal can release a Christian athlete's potential in every practice session and competition. Only one goal can make you desire to run wind sprints with an all-out effort when your body screams for relief. It is not a self-satisfying goal, although there is much pleasure involved. The perfect goal focuses your attention on God rather than yourself.

God's athletic goal for you is to conform you to the same likeness as Jesus Christ through your athletic performance. —**Handbook on Athletic Perfection**

KINGDOM SPORTS MINUTE

SCAN ME

MOTIVATION

EYES ON THE RIGHT KINGDOM

1. Why do you play or coach sports? (Choose all that apply)

- ❏ I'm competitive and I like to win.

- ❏ Sports are a great way to have fun.

- ❏ I love the sport I play/coach.

- ❏ Sports are a way that I can honor Jesus.

- ❏ I want to be part of a team.

- ❏ Sports can help me become more like Jesus.

- ❏ Athletes/coaches tend to be popular.

- ❏ I can use sports as a platform to share Jesus.

- ❏ Sports allow me to have a positive influence on others.

- ❏ My parents/friends want me to play sports.

2. Would you say that your motivations to participate in sports tend to come from a positive or a negative place? Why do you think that is the case?

WHAT'S MY MOTIVATION?

That's a big question which might have different answers throughout your life. Some goals are achieved quickly, perhaps even daily, while others are accomplished over months, years, or even a lifetime.

That question is typically something an actor might ask the director when rehearsing his or her lines. It's an important factor as they hone their craft and prepare to give the best performance possible.

But the question of motivation is far more important to internally ask yourself in everyday life:

• What gets you out of bed in the morning?

• What keeps you showing up for school?

• What motivates you to go to work?

• What inspires you to contribute to your local church, your local community, and society at large?

For the competitive coach or athlete, some healthy motivations might be to stay physically active, to be part of a team, to learn life lessons, or to have a positive impact on others.

Unfortunately, far too many athletic motivations come from an unhealthy and negative mindset: personal recognition, personal satisfaction, pleasing others, proving people wrong, revenge, anger and, perhaps the root cause of them all, fear.

When fear is the primary motivator (fear of failure, fear of what others think, fear of insignificance, fear of loss, etc.), everything you do will be circum-stance-based and dependent solely on performance.

But when operating within a biblical worldview, our motivation as competitors (just like our Goal) should always be based on conforming to Christ. Whatever motivated Him during His life and ministry on the earth should also be what motivates us as we work out our Christian faith as athletes and coaches.

"My nourishment comes from doing the will of God, who sent me, and from finishing His work." (John 4:34)

In John chapter 4, Jesus used a physiological metaphor about the human's need for food to explain to His disciples what motivated Him was to complete the work God had sent Him to do.

Just like Jesus, our competitive motivation (and our motivation for everything else we do in life) should also be driven by a desire to do God's will and receive the ultimate reward for being faithful to the work we've been called to do (see Philippians 3:14).

Yes, there are positive motivations that can drive us in competition, but if they are not rooted in Christ-focused goals, those motivations will ultimately fall short in our quest to experience the fullness of Divine purpose. That's why it's so important to understand what the Word of God has to say.

In the Doing Sports God's Way book, we'll examine some key motivations that will help us align God's perfect "why"(Motivation) with His perfect "what" (Goal). Those motivations are the Gospel, Faith, Worship, and Witness.

Before diving in, however, take some time to further assess what you currently believe about the intersection of motivations for athletic goals and God's call to conformity to Christ:

1. Do you believe that you've always had pure competitive motivations? Explain.

2. How often does fear drive your athletic performance?

3. Does fear as a motivator seem to be A) highly effective, B) mostly effective, C) sometimes effective or D) never effective? Explain.

4. How do you think conforming to Christ might have an impact on your competitive motivations?

KINGDOM CONNECTION

You can express your love for God through your athletic performance. The apostle Paul wrote that, as a Christian, you can use your physical abilities, which include your athletic performance, to unleash your love for God. He wrote, "I urge you, therefore, brethren, by the mercies of God (because of how God demonstrated His love for you on the cross), to present your bodies (consciously commit your physical abilities to God), a living and holy sacrifice (dead to your own interests and alive to God's interests) acceptable to God, which is your spiritual service of worship (the most logical way for you to express your love and reverence to God)" (Romans 12:1). —**Handbook on Athletic Perfection**

KINGDOM SPORTS MINUTE

SCAN ME

STRATEGY

EYES ON THE RIGHT PATH

1. As an athlete or coach, what strategies do you employ to prepare yourself to give your best during competition?

2. Is it enough to be faithful (train hard, practice hard, play hard) and trust God for the results or do you think He expects you to be successful too? Explain.

WHAT IS YOUR STRATEGY?

It's the million-dollar question. How do you get to a place where you are competing at peak levels as an athlete or coach? That's a question that must be answered or you may never reach your full potential.

For some athletes, it's all about physical and mental training. For others, it's fueled by going all out during practice or getting in lots of reps on the field, on the court, on the mat, or on the track.

Coaches might spend hours in the film room or the meeting room assessing the competition and devising game plans. In other words, there are some very clear strategies that will give a team or an individual the best chance at achieving a desired outcome.

But, for the Christian competitor, the question is even more complex. You know what you need to do (the goal). You know why you need to do it (the motivation). But how in the world do you get loose from the bondage of circumstance-based, fear-based, and performance-based competition and release yourself into a higher realm of untapped potential and unfettered worship?

Mercifully, God hasn't asked you do something that sometimes seems impossible without an instruction guide—a strategy, if you will—to lead you down the path to freedom within a broken sports culture. That's because He always wants what it best for His children.

There are many biblical stories that show how God gives His followers a strategy for physical, material, and, most importantly, spiritual success. There is no better example than in the life of Jesus Christ who demonstrated what that looked like. He emptied Himself (see Philippians 2:5-7) and became human flesh to show the importance of relying solely on the Holy Spirit, which filled Him up and gave Him the power to overcome temptation and the wisdom to share the gospel and disciple His followers.

The Old Testament prophet Isaiah caught a glimpse of how Jesus would use these divine strategies to change the world—hundreds of years before His arrival on planet Earth.

The Spirit of the Sovereign Lord is upon me,

> **for the Lord has anointed me**

> **to bring good news to the poor.**

He has sent me to comfort the brokenhearted

> **and to proclaim that captives will be released**

> **and prisoners will be freed. (Isaiah 61:1/NLT)**

As athletes and coaches, it may seem impossible sometimes to walk in unity with the Holy Spirit and conform to the image of Christ, especially while living in a culture that is so self-reliant and self-absorbed.

In the Doing Sports God's Way book, however, we'll take a look at three specific strategies that Jesus modeled while on earth (Prayer, God's Word, and Fellowship) that will help us become the Christ-following competitor that God has called us to become. We'll also take a look at Focal Points, an effective strategy for **Doing Sports God's Way** in the heat of competition.

1. How important do you think it is for a Christian to be strategic in his or her spiritual life: A) critically important, B) somewhat important, C) not very important or D) not important at all? Explain.

2. What strategies do you employ as you seek to conform to the image of Christ?

3. How consistent are you in sticking to those strategies and in what ways have you seen them produce positive results in your life?

4. What has typically happened in those times when you weren't consistent in employing a strategy for spiritual success?

KINGDOM CONNECTION

You have a responsibility to invest your athletic abilities for His purpose! Jesus told a story about the use of talents in Matthew 25:14–30. He was talking about money but the truth applies to any raw talent God gives. It includes your athletic abilities. This was his Master's statement: "The man who uses well what he is given shall be given more, and he shall have abundance. But from the man who is unfaithful, even what little responsibility he has shall be taken away from him" (Matthew 25:29, The Living Bible).

You have been given physical and mental abilities for a purpose. God expects you to invest wisely the talents you do have.—**Handbook on Athletic Perfection**

KINGDOM SPORTS MINUTE

SCAN ME

SUCCESS

EYES ON THE RIGHT OUTCOME

1. Which of the following fit in your current description of what it means to win as an athlete or coach (check all that apply)?

- ❏ Becoming the champion (conference, state, etc.)

- ❏ Breaking a record

- ❏ Defeating your opponent

- ❏ Earning a scholarship

- ❏ Getting/keeping your job/starting position

- ❏ Having more wins than losses

- ❏ Leading a player or teammate to Christ

- ❏ Making a positive impact on those around you

2. Do you find yourself mostly thinking about material success in athletics or personal impact? Explain.

WHAT IS WINNING?

In our sports culture, the answer to the question is as a simple as a quick glance at the scoreboard. Winning is all about the trophy case, the championships, the records, the scholarships, the contracts, the endorsements, and the accolades.

Even though a small percentage of athletes and coaches will ever experience the highest levels of success, we still place all of those hard-to-attain things at the apex of the competitive sports world.

But what if true athletic success has little to do with those material things and everything to do with a much higher calling?

As we've already discussed in the section on Goal, your first priority as a believer is to conform to the image of Christ in all aspects of life (athletics included). Then, winning becomes the total release of all you are toward the goal of becoming like Christ in every situation.

Work willingly at whatever you do, as though you were working for the Lord rather than for people. (Colossians 3:23/NLT)

On the flipside, losing is not releasing your entire self toward becoming like Christ in every situation.

In other words, it's not about the scoreboard. It's about the condition of your heart. It's about who you are competing for and not about material goals you are competing to achieve. It's about our number one goal of dying to self, conforming to the image of Christ and trusting in Him for the outcomes (see Galatians 2:20). That's winning! That's success!

But that doesn't mean we shouldn't do our best and make an effort to be competitive on the playing field. It just means success in the world's eyes looks a lot different than success in God's eyes—and at the end of the day, winning and losing in the traditional sense will take care of itself.

When we have a biblical worldview on competitive success and the rewards that often follow, it's always a good idea to remember what Jesus had to say about the matter:

"Don't store up treasures here on earth, where moths eat them and rust destroys them, and where thieves break in and steal. Store your treasures in heaven, where moths and rust cannot destroy, and thieves do not break in and steal. Wherever your treasure is, there the desires of your heart will also be." (Matthew 6:19-21/NLT)

In the Doing Sports God's Way book, we will take a look at four ways to judge whether or not you have a biblical worldview on competitive success: Confidence in Identity, Intensity in Focus, Endurance in Competition, and Contentment in Competition.

1. How do you think the world's definition of winning and losing may have hindered your athletic performance?

2. How has God's definition of winning and losing helped your athletic performance?

3. What do you think it looks like to have a total release of your abilities while competing for God and not men?

4. How close do you feel like you've come to achieving a total release of your abilities?

5. What are some things that might be holding you back from doing so?

KINGDOM CONNECTION

Winning is the total release of all that you are toward becoming like Jesus Christ in each situation. Losing is not releasing your entire self toward becoming like Jesus Christ in each situation.

What a difference this is from the long ingrained definition of winning and losing. When you have God's perspective on winning and losing, circumstances will not control your athletic performance.—**Handbook on Athletic Perfection**

KINGDOM SPORTS MINUTE

SCAN ME